HANGING OUT A SHINGLE

HANGING OUT A SHINGLE

An Insider's Guide
to Starting
Your Own Law Firm

Harry F. Weyher

Foreword by
Charles S. Lyon,
Gerald L. Wallace Professor of Taxation,
New York University School of Law

DODD, MEAD & COMPANY
NEW YORK

A GAMUT BOOK

Published by Dodd, Mead & Company, Inc.
71 Fifth Avenue, New York, N.Y. 10003
Manufactured in the United States of America
Designed by Joyce Levatino
First Edition

1 2 3 4 5 6 7 8 9 10

Library of Congress Cataloging-in-Publication Data

Weyher, Harry F.
  Hanging out a shingle.

  Includes index.
  1. Law offices—United States. 2. Law firms—United
States. I. Title.
KF318.Z9W49 1987   338.7'6134   87-19937
ISBN 0-396-08984-4
ISBN 0-396-09196-2 {PBK}

CONTENTS

Foreword vii
Acknowledgments xi
Preface xiii

Chapter 1 WHY START YOUR OWN FIRM? 1
*Those who have started their own firms, large
and small, because of altruism, greed, ambition,
or the pursuit of pleasure.*

Chapter 2 YOUR FIRST CLIENTS 10
Starting out small; building a client list.

Chapter 3 WHERE TO SET UP SHOP? 28
*What kind of practice do you want? How to
set your goals intelligently.*

Chapter 4 CHOOSING A PARTNER—OR
GOING IT ALONE 38
Advantages and disadvantages.

Chapter 5 HOW MUCH TO CHARGE 57
Fair fees, fair profits.

Chapter 6 PEOPLE, EQUIPMENT, AND
OTHER ESSENTIALS 71
*Finding the right place; choosing the
right people.*

Chapter 7 GENERAL PRACTICE 88
Arguments for and against specialization.

Chapter 8 LITIGATION PRACTICE 101
*Is the courtroom ready for you? Arguments
for and against.*

Chapter 9 TAX PRACTICE 115
*The inevitability of death and taxes.
Possibilities and pitfalls of tax law.*

Chapter 10   CORPORATE PRACTICE   127
Are you a corporate type? Big business as client or adversary

Chapter 11   WOMEN IN THE LAW   137
Is the law business sexist? How the times they are a-changing.

Chapter 12   LOOKING TO THE FUTURE   149
Growing big or staying small? Realistic planning.

FOREWORD

Back in 1948, before I went to Washington to work for the government and before I became a law school professor, three friends and I started a law firm of our own. I was to be the tax partner.

We started it from scratch, with no big clients as a base. Still we started optimistically to hire an associate. I went along with this idea because if we didn't need him within a year we would be going under anyway. We contacted faculty members we knew at Harvard Law School about a great opportunity, with a brand-new law firm! The result was a chubby associate, soon to graduate from Harvard. In retrospect we were still a flyspeck of a law firm.

Things went slowly for us—so slowly especially as to tax practice, that after two years I left for government service in Washington. It seemed the best thing at the time, so I did it. Then I went on to teaching.

Harry Weyher's book makes me recall those early years when the four of us—and the single associate—were trying to establish our own law practice. It was exciting and somewhat frightening.

Each new client, even small ones, brought a new thrill. Nothing is more exhilarating—except perhaps collecting a suitable fee from that new client.

This book brings it all back to me. *Hanging Out a Shingle* is a realistic, down-to-earth description of the problems and opportunities facing lawyers of all ages as they embark on their own law practices. It is informative, personable, and readable; and it conveys the humor and humanity in the life of a lawyer.

For some readers this guide will be a lively, informal, practical how-to book; it should be enormously helpful to those about to take the plunge into their own practices. Every law student and prelaw student, as well as every older attorney who is thinking of starting his or her own practice, should read this book.

As a matter of fact, everyone who has contact with lawyers seems to be curious about how they get to be the way they are. This book provides some answers. It shows both Wall Street and down-home lawyers doing their own things in their own special ways.

What about my own start-up law firm?

The four-man firm I helped to establish in 1948 was called Skadden, Arps, Slate & Lyon; the last name was mine. They dropped my name when I went into government service and later added two others—Meagher and Flom. Now it has more than 700 lawyers. Last year the firm reportedly billed over $225 million to its clients.

That chubby young associate is thinner now. His name is Joe Flom, and he is a living legend in the history of building law firms.

Joe Flom, the associate who later helped so much to build my old firm to its present position of greatness, and Harry Weyher, who wrote this book, were incidentally classmates and good friends at Harvard Law School.

Of course, not every firm will illustrate Harry Weyher's optimistic view of chances of a new law firm on such a grand scale. But you never can tell.

Charles S. Lyon,
Gerald L. Wallace
Professor of Taxation,
New York University, School of Law

ACKNOWLEDGMENTS

I asked Lee Stern to edit this manuscript with me, as I have on other occasions. As usual, he was super.

Cynthia Vartan oversaw things for the publisher, and anyone is lucky to work with her.

Janet Magnuson coordinated the manuscript and prevented the disintegration of the project, which otherwise would easily have occurred.

PREFACE

A couple of years ago a "raider" took over one of our corporate clients by means of a hostile tender offer. Within three months, in a move that is becoming more common each day, the raider had discharged nine of the ten lawyers on our client's legal staff.

Nine good lawyers, their ages ranging from thirty-two to fifty-eight, were suddenly without jobs. What were they to do?

Only one went to work for another corporation. One retired. One became an investment banker; another became a minister.

Five proudly announced that they had started their own law practices.

I had lunch one day with the lawyer who had taken the corporate job. I asked about those latter five lawyers.

"I feel sorry for them," he said. "Trying to start a law practice from scratch is a terrible risk, especially if you're forty or fifty years old—but maybe also if you're thirty."

He doodled on his napkin, then wrote and handed me a jingle.

> *Here's to lawyers young and old*
> *Who hang out shingles, names in gold,*
> *And wait to find if dice so rolled*
> *Will end their tumbles hot or cold.*

Dice? Is it really that kind of risk—a roll of the dice?

These were our friends he was discussing. His attitude worried me. What could they hope for or expect?

During the next year I spent time with all five of the new entrepreneurs. I also talked to my own law school classmates and to other lawyers. I asked all of them about the perils and pleasures of starting one's own law practice.

It didn't seem that dicey to me. After all, I had helped start my own firm with three other young partners years before, when I was four years out of law school, and I never regretted it.

Before long, I came to realize that many more lawyers than I had imagined are starting their own practices every year. The statistics are staggering. Many are fresh out of law school. Some are middle-aged. Some are old by corporate standards.

Statistically, the chances of success are good, although I've distrusted bald statistics ever since someone told me of the statistician who drowned in a creek with an average depth of one and a half feet. The analogy to dice is just plain bad. At dice, there are 976 chances of a pass, or a win, as against 1004 chances of losing—or 49.25 percent—at least at honest private crap games.

Out of the hundreds of lawyers I know about who have started their own practices, I don't know one who considers the decision a total loss. Some did better than others, but the difference is in the degree of success. Some found that the new income was inadequate for their needs and gave up their practice for greener fields or seemingly better opportunities. But not one of my acquaintances failed totally. Not one was forced to file for bankruptcy or the equivalent. The odds of *some* degree of success are almost a hundred to zero.

So I estimate, based on these acquaintances' experiences, that the chances of *substantial* success are very good, at least if one does a little advance study and learns what he or she will face and what to expect.

Beyond the lure of the financial reward is the personal satisfaction of creating the practice, the reveling in your own personal achievement. And there is also the freedom of being your own boss. Each professional success is *your* success, not that of some employer. There is also freedom from restrictive work rules. And you have your choice of clients and coworkers. There are many advantages other than financial.

Eventually I decided to set forth in this book what I had learned about starting your own law firm, the decisions to be made, the problems to be faced, the payoffs to be had.

I hope this book will be helpful to law students, lawyers leaving corporations, and ex-government lawyers who are thinking of starting their own firms. I hope it is helpful to younger people who are debating whether to go to law school. And I hope and believe it may be interesting to nonlawyers who are fascinated by the lives and exploits of attorneys, who are increasingly a part of everybody's life.

This book is too late to help my five friends who lost their jobs a couple of years ago and started their own law practices. But then, they don't need help. Their new practices are successful.

Harry F. Weyher

1

WHY START YOUR OWN FIRM?

This book is about lawyers who practice law on their own—who start their own law firms.

Why do they do it? How? What is it like?

Every year, literally thousands of people with law degrees—perhaps hundreds of thousands—consider starting their own law firms.

Some do it because they're ambitious; others because they're greedy; still others because they like the idea of freedom. Some find it exciting. Some can't get jobs and have no other choice. The reasons are infinite. Some even start their own practice out of altruism.

Look at Clarence Darrow, who became America's most famous trial lawyer and was later portrayed in the play and movie *Inherit the Wind*. Darrow decided to quit his job as a railroad attorney and open a one-man law practice just to help Eugene V. Debs in his labor crusade.

Darrow wrote:

I stood on the prairie watching the burning [railroad] cars.
. . . The railroads asked the Federal Court for injunctions.

> ... When I saw poor men giving up their jobs for a cause, I could find no sufficient excuse, except my selfish interest, for refusing. ... And so I gave up my position and became one of the attorneys for Mr. Debs in the great strike of the American Railway Union. ... In 1894 I opened an office and went into private practice.

Darrow became the protagonist in some of the landmark cases of American history, including not only the *Eugene V. Debs* railroad strike case (involving the right to strike against the government), but also the *Scopes* "monkey trial" (in which the teaching of evolution was vindicated) and the *Leopold Loeb* murder case (in which the temporary insanity defense was developed). These matters would not be studied in law schools today if it weren't for one man, Clarence Darrow.

Of course, everyone would like to become rich or famous or both after opening an office, but many have other motivations as well. Some attorneys simply long for independence. Some can't find another job. Some desperately want to leave the job they now have. Some have just lost a job—perhaps because of a corporate takeover. A few have ready-made clients, or they inherit the legal work for a family business. Others evolve into independence after doing part-time legal work at night. They may open their own offices with enthusiasm and a good future, without realistic hope of riches or fame.

Sometimes your own personal legal problems can propel you into starting a law firm. After Richard Greenfield received his law degree from Cornell in 1967, he went to work for Villager Industries, a Philadelphia women's clothing company. He received stock in the company. Greenfield says he was at first dazzled by the high salary, limousines, and perks, but that soon he came to believe that the company was misstating its inventories in connection with a sale of stock by the chairman. He thought about going to the Securities and Exchange Commission with his suspicions but decided to resign instead, to get away from the questionable activities and to start his own law practice.

He furnished an office in his own house and started a general practice in wills, estates, divorces, and real estate. One of his principal personal assets was the Villager stock. But its market value went down at a time when his fledging law practice was barely supporting him. So he went to a Philadelphia attorney, Harold Kohn, of Kohn, Savett, Marion & Graf. Kohn was so impressed by Greenfield's story that he brought a class action against Villager, which eventually was settled in 1972 by payment to the stockholders—including Greenfield—of $2.7 million.

Greenfield was so fascinated by the lawsuit and by Kohn's handling of it that he immediately decided to specialize—in his own solo practice—in cases of a similar type, securities cases. There was quick success. Today his one-man practice has evolved into the eight-partner firm of Greenfield & Chimicles in a Philadelphia suburb. It concentrates on securities law matters, almost exclusively for plaintiffs, on a contingent fee basis. It is feared or maybe hated by defendant corporations.

The Greenfield firm has developed, in one way or another, such a large inventory of cases—particularly against stockbrokers and companies issuing stock—that settlements occur with some regularity, and even though all the fees are contingent, the cash flow is remarkably smooth. This firm, which arose from legal indiscretions by Villager Industries observed by one of its own employees, has been successful enough to be profiled in *USA Today*, *The Philadelphia Inquirer*, *The American Lawyer*, and *The Wall Street Journal*. It has been mentioned extensively, if gingerly, in *Investment Dealers' Digest*.

Many lawyers consider starting their own firms but do nothing; others delay and delay, only to reconsider year after year.

Who are all these people?

First, 35,000 graduates flow out of law schools each year. Preceding them were some 750,000 law school graduates now in various kinds of employment—some in government, some with businesses. More than 450,000 are in law practice, and gross about $35 billion in annual fees. *Barron's Guide to Law Schools* gives the initial employment breakdown for 300,000 graduates of the 1974–82 classes as follows.

Private practice	54%
Public interest	5%
Business	10%
Government	15%
Judicial clerkship	10%
Military	2%
Academic	3%
Other	1%

That's what happens just after law school. After some shifting later on, business employment grows to about 20 percent of all lawyers. Any way you slice it, there are a lot of lawyers out there, and many estimate that there will be more than 1 million by the year 2000. On a per capita basis, the United States has over twice as many lawyers per thousand people as England, five times as many as West Germany, and twenty-five times as many as Japan.

There are three-quarters of a million lawyers in this country! President Derek Bok of Harvard has asked whether there isn't too great a concentration of American brain power in the legal field, at the expense of the sciences, academia, and other essential occupations. President Bok's view is shared by a man who says of his divorce that "there were lawyers everywhere—hundreds of them, all trying to ruin me." That may be an exaggeration, but only a slight one, at least from his perspective.

As these lawyers move along their professional paths, some decide to make career changes; others are forced to change careers after being "passed over" by law firms or pushed out of other jobs. Many of these flood their résumés onto law firms, corporations, and government departments. Some cannot get jobs because of a lack of proper qualifications, others because of a lack of suitable jobs. Discouraged, many of these resort to opening their own law practices. Others, more confident, turn earlier toward opening their own shops. The size of the pool of new entrepreneurial lawyers each year cannot be estimated, but it numbers conservatively in the tens of thousands.

Forbes, in its January 16, 1984, issue, summarized the law of supply and demand—or at least the law of supply—as follows:

Russell Howes was graduated from Wayne State University law school in 1980 expecting immediate success, the kind his older brother enjoyed in the Sixties. After applying to over 150 law firms without one offer, Howes is chastened. "The opportunities have dried up," he explains. "In any major city you're considered a golden boy if you're able to snare a job." Howes launched his own practice in a small Michigan town a couple of months ago. But this, too, is discouraging. "Someone comes through the door about every week and a half," he says.

Freshly graduated attorneys aren't the only ones with problems. . . . Several large firms have gone out of business. Marshall, Bratter, Greene, Allison & Tucker, a 100-lawyer New York City firm with fancy Park Avenue offices, closed its doors in 1982. So did Greenbaum, Wolff & Ernst, a specialist in the literary field. More recently, a well-known entertainment firm, Fulop & Hardee, fell apart.

Even large in-house legal staffs are feeling the pinch. One middle-aged attorney, for example, left his job as group counsel at a division of a Forbes 500 company two years ago after a corporate restructuring. With Ivy League degrees and 20 years' experience, he thought he would find a job quickly. "But I was wrong," he says today—still unemployed.

These are common reasons for starting a new law firm.

Sometimes there are uncommon ones.

In the nineteenth century John Wesley Harding shot 44 men in the Old West and then opened a law office, presumably because his prior business had been too highly specialized and he wanted to broaden his career opportunities.

Abraham Lincoln in 1837 formed a two-man partnership in Springfield with John T. Stuart in order to handle the latter's business while Stuart was running for Congress. Lincoln himself followed the traveling judge by horse from county to county over the Eighth Circuit while Stuart was not politicking and could stay home and mind the office.

Going back farther in time, Daniel Webster opened his own law practice so that he would be free to go hunting and fishing whenever he pleased, which was often—at least when he wasn't a Senator or Secretary of State. (It is said that he also wanted a little more free time for food and drink.)

Ralph C. Goldman founded a highly successful and exciting divorce firm in New York, providing that vital service to many socialites and celebrities. His former firm had decided to stop handling divorce work and tried to get Goldman to specialize in real estate law, which he detested, so he simply hung out his own shingle.

Peter Megaree Brown formed a two-man partnership with Whitney North Seymour, Jr., to practice law "like a gentleman"—presumably in contrast to both men's experiences at large New York firms.

Walter S. Carter, known as the "collector of young masters"—brilliant young associate lawyers—moved from Chicago in 1871 and formed a firm in New York, saying that the Midwest had too many lawyers.

Maryanne LaGuardia, one of the few "big-asset Hollywood divorce lawyers," left a fifty-person law firm to found a divorce practice with a small firm. She says that her reasons were "greed and power," higher earnings, and greater esteem.

Nicholas Chase left his partnership with Edward Bennett Williams in Washington and went his own way, it is said, because Chase wanted first to believe in the "justice" of a client's cause, whereas Williams was determined first to win the case.

United States Supreme Court Justice Sandra Day O'Connor, third in her class at Stanford in the days before women were acceptable in law firms, was offered a job as a legal secretary and could not get a job as a lawyer. So she opened a "neighborhood law office" in Arizona with another woman; the two of them dealt with "every . . . problem that would come in the door."

Tom Ellis formed his own law firm in Raleigh so that he would be free to devote some time to politics. This enabled him to mastermind the election of two Republican United States senators in a normally Democratic state.

In 1869, the major reason the most successful criminal firm in the nation's history, Howe & Hummel, was formed was that neither of these two pioneers could have found a respectable lawyer for a partner. They stayed together until 1907, when the district attorney closed the firm for various malpractices. Howe was disbarred for attempting to bribe a judge and then was reinstated before he died; Hummel was convicted, disbarred, and jailed after the Texas Rangers closed in on a key witness that Hummel had hidden away in Louisiana and Texas brothels.

More later about some of these lawyers.

A few words of caution: "The best laid schemes o' mice and men gang aft a-gley." And so it is with your decision to start a law practice—it might get derailed.

Jay Finnegan set a schedule for himself: graduate in June 1985 from NYU Law School, a June and July bar review course, an August bar exam for New York, a December passing grade on the bar exam and filing for admission to the bar, a January 1986 swearing in, and the simultaneous opening of his own law office with a classmate, John O'Hara. Every step was precisely laid out. They found desirable office space, selected furniture, and began negotiating a lease to commence in January.

The NYU graduation happened right on schedule. The June and July bar review course happened right on schedule. The bar exam happened right on schedule.

O'Hara's phone rang on Thursday, August 8, 1985. It was Finnegan.

"Stop that lease! Hold everything. They've really screwed me."

"What's the matter?"

"I just got a call!" yelled Finnegan. "The damned Board of Law Examiners lost our bar exams. My exam paper is lost or stolen, and everybody else's, too. I'm screwed!"

And so he was. The test papers of 542 people who took the New York bar exam at a location known as Pier 90 had been lost or stolen—they were gone from a locked office at 270 Broadway!

He was so near to his new law firm, and yet so far.

("I wish *my* paper had been lost," said a discouraged law student who took the bar exam elsewhere.)

Deciding to go it alone, to forsake the protective umbrella of a large corporation or an established law firm, is not easy. Only you can make the ultimate decision about whether you possess the requisite amounts of nerve, money, contacts, and ambition. Unfortunately, talent isn't enough, as many have learned to their chagrin.

The following chapters discuss the real-life questions you will face as you start and maintain your own law practice. They will suggest answers to these questions and ways to avoid the problems. They will tell you about attorneys who have started their own firms—their triumphs, disappointments, victories, and defeats—and the lessons they learned along the way. Hard lessons learned by others may help you avoid errors on your way to establishing and maintaining your own law practice.

You may never become rich or famous, but there's always a chance you can become both. The only guarantee is that, although you may sometimes be frustrated and often exasperated, if you possess the right legal stuff you'll never be bored.

◆◆◆◆◆◆◆

Why not start your own law firm?

It sounds like an easy decision, but it requires a huge amount of thought. You've read in this chapter true tales of attorneys who *did* make the big decision, their various reasons for doing so, and the outcome of their actions. Remember that wonderful title, *Do You Sincerely Want to Be Rich?* Well, a sincere wish to be rich or famous or both is not enough.

Talent and ambition are necessary, too, but they aren't enough either. You must also possess the nerve, the perseverance, and sometimes connections and luck to make your own firm successful. And you will need careful planning.

Even if you decide that you do sincerely want to be relatively independent, there are still many other decisions to confront.

How do you get your first clients? Would you prefer to practice in a small town or in a big city? Should you seek a partner or go it alone? How much should you charge for the services you'll perform? Do you want to handle anything that comes your way, or do you want to specialize? If you *do* specialize, will you feel more at home in a courtroom or a boardroom? Is your sex—male or female—likely to be an advantage or a disadvantage? Would you prefer to retain the warm intimacy of a small practice, or would you like to see your office grow into a huge factory-type firm?

These and other vital questions will be addressed in the remaining chapters of this book. You will find explanations, discussions, and dialectics. But only you can answer all these questions from the viewpoint of your own lifestyle, personality, and objectives.

This book provides food for careful thought.

After that, it's up to you.

2

YOUR FIRST CLIENTS

So you've decided you want to start out on your own. You're convinced you have the attributes and the ambition to make it. The next step, in practical terms, might be to find an office, hire a secretary, buy reference books, and perform many other dull but necessary tasks. But in terms of your anxiety about the venture, the question of *how to get clients* probably looms much larger. So let's talk about that first.

Of course, if you've just left a law firm, you may bring some clients with you when you start your new practice. But that is rare. Most lawyers starting out don't have a proven client base—only hopes or maybe prayers that old contacts will turn into clients.

Imagine sitting in a new office hour after hour, day after day, waiting for the first client. Maybe, if things are going badly, you're biting your nails and waiting for the phone to ring, week after week. When it does, you think to yourself, Will clients know I'm just starting out? Will they know I'm inexperienced in matters like this? Will they think I'm too young? Too old? Too small, without a large supporting staff? Too presumptuous? Will they know that I don't have any other clients?

When these doubts cross your mind—and they will—just remember that although you are a lawyer without any clients, the potential client is a client without any lawyer.

Why *doesn't* he have a lawyer already? Is he a criminal too dastardly for others to represent—maybe even a child rapist? Or did he skip out on his previous lawyers without paying them? Will he pay you? Or is she trying to get you to lend your unsullied reputation and good name to a fraudulent scheme of some sort?

As these questions about the client run through your head, you will get things into a better focus. You'll realize that doubts exist in both directions, and you'll be able to face the meeting with less apprehension. It's not a one-sided affair. There must be some reason the client needs you, maybe even more than you need the client.

When the critical moment arrives, be careful to let the prospective client tell the full story. Be sure, when you've finished, that you have gotten it all. Don't jump to conclusions.

One of my first clients, maybe the very first, was a man named Bill Ewing. After calling me late the night before, he came into my office—I could smell drink still on his breath—bearing an angry look and an angry voice. I asked what I might do for him.

"My wife," he rasped. "She's run away, the bitch!"

I sensed an opportunity. "I have a good knowledge of divorce law from a seminar I went to. We'll win the divorce suit."

"No! No! It's not a divorce I'm after," he said. "Let me continue. When she left, she rented a van and stole my prize horse. She's taken him to California, the bitch!"

"Oh, now I see," I said eagerly. "I'll research that tonight and see if we can replevin the horse from California. I learned a little about that in my course on English common law, and I'm sure I can help you get the horse back."

"No! No! Stop interrupting me, counselor," said Ewing. "I'm not after the horse that the bitch stole. The horse was lame."

Confused, I said, "I see, I see."

I waited, and then I asked, "Why are you here?"

"That's what I'm getting to, counselor," he explained. "When the bitch stole my horse, she didn't tell the stable that he wouldn't be back. Now they've sent me a livery bill for three months of feeding and stabling, and the horse wasn't even there."

I was nervous about claiming expertise in a third field of law within such a short interview, but I managed to mumble something under my breath about hearing of livery stables in Western movies. I said aloud that I now understood.

This case eventually worked out about as you might expect. The stable reduced its bill a small amount, and Ewing paid the balance angrily. I sent him a bill for a fraction of my time, since anything else would have been larger than the reduction in the livery bill. Ewing became a long-term client and later became involved in larger and more lucrative legal problems. My first-client jitters were behind me.

I should add that I now let people finish their stories before I comment on their problems and brag about my knowledge.

How do you get the first client to come in? The conventional ways are to hang out a shingle (if you are in a small town), to mail out announcements, and above all to tell all your friends (and enemies, too) that you are in business.

I guarantee that business will come. It may not be good business; it might even be business you'd rather not have. But it will be there. And you can't predict why.

Senator Sam J. Ervin, Jr., of North Carolina tells the story of his beginnings in *Humor of a Country Lawyer*.

I am indebted to [my father and a friend] for my acquiring a considerable practice as a trial lawyer soon after I hung out my shingle. . . . Their endeavors were enhanced by the circumstance that I was compelled to absent myself from the first week of the August term of the superior court of Burke County to attend the summer encampment of the North Carolina National Guard. Retired emergency judge C. C. Lyon, of distant Bladen County, had been assigned to hold a one week session of the August term, which was designed to try criminal cases.

In as much as Judge Lyon was unknown to Burke County sinners and they were hesitant to confront uncertainty of punishment, and they thought he would be gone the following week, all of them who had cases scheduled for trial asserted I was their lawyer and asked the court to postpone their trials until the next week so they could be defended by me. Judge Lyon acceded to their requests and recessed court for the week, saying that it was the only time he had been compelled to adjourn court and stay over himself because of the absence of one lawyer.

Since all of them had assured the court that I was their attorney, they were necessarily compelled to retain my services before they confronted Judge Lyon during the recessed session the second week.

Senator Sam's experience was not unique. Carl Sandburg says of Abraham Lincoln that "murderers, horse thieves, scandalmongers, and slanderers came at various times and poured out their stories amid the walls of" his new law office in Springfield. Sandburg probably could have added crackpots, since they appear periodically in all law offices.

In many instances, of course, and perhaps in most cases, a new lawyer is averse to the practice of criminal law, divorce, and other such sordid matters. If you are that sensitive, how do you attract other kinds of business, such as corporations, syndicates, and estates?

In earlier years, there was little you could do except surreptitiously spread the word that you were an expert in this field or that. A few flamboyant lawyers like Louis Nizer, Edward Bennett Williams, and F. Lee Bailey have written books about themselves under the guise of describing cases. But except for this flamboyant self-publicity, lawyers could not advertise. They could not even permit a magazine or newspaper to write an unsolicited favorable story about them if they were aware that it was being written. I and three other senior partners of my own firm, Olwine, Connelly, Chase, O'Donnell & Weyher, were censured in 1963 at the recommendation of the Association of the Bar of the City of New York for an unsolicited article about our firm in *Life* magazine.

But in 1977 the United States Supreme Court declared that publicity and advertising are legal, and then things changed.

Today many law firms advertise; larger ones even have public relations representation. You might, if you want to, try both.

A public relations firm will write speeches for you and try to find a place for you to present the speeches— perhaps on radio or TV. Ditto for magazine articles; maybe even a book like this one (although I take the responsibility for this venture myself). It might arrange for journalists to call you and quote you on various subjects—perhaps on international crises or on Princess Margaret's latest social escapade. It will try to get you listed in *Who's Who* or other biographical books. It will even retouch glossy prints of you, in case the press should need one, and tell you which is your good side. One public relations firm sent a lawyer-client on a big-game hunt in Africa and had movies made of him in heroic poses. (If you do something like this, take along a good professional hunter. If your shot strays into the wrong end of the elephant, you and the public relations person and the movie photographer could find yourselves in extremely deep trouble.)

In earlier days lawyers hired "chasers" to bring in business from automobile crashes, slips on ice, and the like. And chasers got a fee. This probably is now off limits, but isn't a public relations person doing the same thing on a grander scale?

One lone practitioner, John P. Coale of Washington, D.C., rushes to disaster sites himself; he says it is necessary to see and tag the evidence. He flew to Bhopal, India, soon after a poison gas leak at the Union Carbide plant there killed 2,000 people in 1984; he flew to Puerto Rico after a fire at the Dupont Plaza Hotel killed 96 people in 1986. He got no clients from Bhopal because the trial was transferred from the United States to India, but he got plenty of publicity from the trip; he picked up over thirty clients in Puerto Rico.

Many other lawyers have scurried uninvited to disaster sites, such as the Baltimore train crash in 1987 that killed 16 and injured 175 people.

Bar associations frown on rushing to mass disaster sites. But for some lawyers the only constraint is against going to a hospital when victims are being brought in and have not yet had medical aid.

To gather new plaintiffs in asbestosis cases, some lawyers have used direct-mail solicitation of persons who may have been exposed, such as shipyard workers, merchant seamen, workers in tire plants, and sheet metal workers.

Leonard Jacques, a Detroit lawyer, runs a clinic to test merchant seamen. He has filed asbestos claims for 1,500 seamen and plans to test 20,000 more. He solicits by direct mailings. Gordon Stemple, a Los Angeles lawyer, sends vans offering free chest X rays to tire workers in twenty-five states; his partner, Richard F. Gerry of San Diego, foresees 30,000 cases.

Melvin Belli, the "king of torts," likes to twit his critics by saying, "I'm not an ambulance chaser. I've gotten there before the ambulance several times."

As for paid advertising, lawyers today use all types.

About 5,000 firms are said to advertise actively. They spend almost $50 million a year on TV ads alone. That includes cable TV ads for one-person firms; this one now plays many times an hour on Manhattan Cable Classifieds.

PAUL M. FINGERHUT, ATTORNEY
PERSONAL INJURIES, REAL ESTATE CLOSINGS,
LANDLORD AND TENANT.
PERSONAL CONSULTATION BY APPOINTMENT
962-5225

Another lawyer appeared on TV in a scuba diver's wetsuit seeking clients who were "over your head in debt."

In the yellow pages of the Manhattan telephone book, half-page ads hawk all kinds of expertise, free consultations, 24-hour service, Saturday and Sunday appointments, toll-free telephone numbers—you name it. Among the specialties frequently cited in these ads are divorce, drunk driving, birth defects, surgical errors, explosions, slip-and-fall, libel and slander, brain damage, unmarried couples, and squatters.

One ad ominously gives the lawyer's specialty as "doctors"; another boasts of an "attorney with master's degree in psychology." One says "experienced in the recovery of large money awards"; another says "former judge"; another "registered pharmacist." Still another calls himself "the caring lawyer."

An ad headed "Jacoby & Meyers is nearby" is suggestive of daring rescues by the Lone Ranger. It lists five Manhattan locations and a telephone number for finding other locations. Jacoby & Meyers TV ads for handling estates, divorces, and crimes are ubiquitous, delivered in a soft, fatherly, reassuring tone.

Lawyers have issued discount coupons and put their names on billboards and matchbook covers, not to mention on bowling alley scorecards. Glossy brochures abound. Vetter & White of Providence distributes a promotional brochure containing a photo of two nude women in a bathtub; somehow this is supposed to prove their skills at litigation. Seminars are held for potential clients. One lawyer from a major Chicago firm hands prospective clients a memorandum listing all the cases he tried in the previous several years, together with the judges' names and telephone numbers and his adversaries' names and telephone numbers. It describes the dimensions of the cases—not the results.

Some firms distribute newsletters touting themselves. Jones, Day in Cleveland puts its newsletters on videocassettes for its potential clients.

Occasionally promotion pieces are too extravagant. The Minneapolis firm of Robins, Zelle puts out a brochure saying, "Facing Robins Zelle in court is a little like encountering Ghengis Khan on the steppes." Maybe you could portray yourself as Wyatt Earp at the pass or Rambo defeating an entire army of fierce adversaries; but then perhaps that goes too far as well.

A number of years ago a lawyer in Harlem was disciplined for utilizing a twenty-foot neon sign, but today his innovative action would probably be condoned.

A survey commissioned by *The American Bar Association Journal* found that of the 24 percent of attorneys who advertise, the least popular form is the billboard. Only 1 percent of them use the billboard. Maybe neon signs show up better.

One lawyer in a small North Carolina town regularly had himself paged over the loudspeaker at high school baseball games to create the impression of overflowing business.

As you've probably noticed, these are all pitches that any kind of business could depend on; even a shoe store could use TV or a billboard. Why not go a step further and call on prospective clients to make your pitch in person? Quote the client your rates, or contingent fees—whatever you think suits both of you best. Describe your specialties and qualifications.

Many firms are going out and selling their services, just like accounting firms, banks, or cosmetics companies. You're behind the times if you don't.

One Chicago lawyer is now experimenting with a videotape presentation for *potential* litigation based on events mentioned in newspapers and magazines. In his video presentation he assumes what the issues will be in a particular case and makes an impressive address to an imaginary jury. Then he shows this videotape to the potential client mentioned in the press to demonstrate his style, presence, and approach. (Should he add a favorable jury decision, played by actors?)

Here's another idea: Why not go whole hog, and offer to make the first legal business *free*? Offer a will or a contract for nothing, on condition that the prospective client will give you his next business if you perform satisfactorily. It's a come-on, like at county fairs.

A new and growing source of routine cut-rate business is the legal service plans that have sprung up in recent years. For a monthly payment starting at $6.75, the customer is entitled to specified legal services—usually a will, telephone conferences, and a few legal letters. These were originally union plans—a form of insurance—but now they are offered to the public by such companies as Prepaid Legal Services, Montgomery Ward, Amway, and Nationwide Legal Services. About 17 million people are estimated to be covered.

So if you want the business, call on these companies and try to get on their list of approved lawyers.

In Los Angeles the four-lawyer firm of Fazio & Fairchild spends most of its time on ten thousand clients covered by such prepaid plans. Feldman & Kramer, an eight-lawyer firm in Hauppauge, Long Island, also serves a large number of such clients.

A variation on this is a plan called Union Privilege

Legal Services offered by the AFL-CIO to its 13 million members. Lawyers who want more work offer a 30 percent "volume discount" to union members for wills, home purchases, divorces, and criminal work. The union returns the favor by directing prospects to these cooperating lawyers. Get in touch with unions near you; or start such a program with the workers at a local factory, whether there is a union or not.

Of course, all this doesn't sound like the dignified, gracious profession you heard about years ago, when it was gauche to discuss fees directly, when there was no advertising or solicitation. Is the lawyer now operating on the same level as the insurance agent? The stockbroker? The Fuller Brush man? In terms of getting business, the answer is yes.

There is one more tangential sales factor: politics. Lawyers, more than any other professionals, enter politics; many do it to enhance their law practices, to become well known, to earn prestigious titles such as judge or senator, or to appear to have magical powers derived from the political background. Perhaps there is even an implication—often undenied by the beneficiary—that a politician lawyer can fix things at a higher place, or at least that his or her presence might be of help.

In addition, politicians get patronage plums. Courts appoint guardians for minors, trustees in bankruptcy, administrators of intestate estates, and the like; executive branches hire lawyers for a myriad of purposes. For example, the liquidation bureau of the New York State Insurance Department paid $5 million in legal fees in 1985 to about three hundred lawyers or law firms. Think what the total fees must be for the entire state executive branch and for all those state agencies. Much of them go to politically connected lawyers.

And that's just the state. The federal and local governments hire lawyers, too.

Chester A. Arthur, the twenty-first President of the

United States, entered politics and became collector of customs for the Port of New York. That entitled him to a percentage of the fines collected by the Custom House; at the same time he practiced law.

You should not overlook yourself as a prospective client. Atlanta attorney Kathleen Kessler sued the State of Georgia, charging that an appointment to the state Supreme Court bench violated Georgia law. On winning, she submitted a bill to herself as a plaintiff under a civil rights law for her services as a lawyer; she was awarded a fee of $70,000.

Why do all this? You may have thought that you would win potential clients over if you play golf with them and let them win by a small margin. Or in a big city, take them to night clubs. In the Caribbean, take them fishing. Anywhere, you might treat them to a gracious dinner or to a sold-out football game, or give them expensive wine at Christmas.

All these things may help a little in getting a client— but only a little. These things may open an office door for a serious pitch, and they do help solidify personal relations with existing clients. But they do not in themselves bring business.

In the early days of my own firm, the Olwine firm, I once reviewed how we had obtained significant clients for the first fifteen years. Perhaps 10 percent could be traced to social connections or to family connections, or they couldn't be traced at all.

But fully 90 percent—that's nine out of ten—came from one source.

What was it? It was recommendations or observations based on other work we had done. It was hearing of us, directly or indirectly, from an existing client or being involved somehow in a matter we were handling for someone else. If we did a good job on a merger or acquisition, people would see it or hear of it sooner or later. If our litigation department did a good job on a particular case, others with similar cases would learn of it and call us. It was referral and references. It was word of mouth.

That is equally true for smaller matters, in which the new client is an individual. It is certainly true—doubly true—when the new client is a corporation with its own internal legal department. Corporate legal departments more and more eschew taking all their work to outside "general counsel." In fact, the outside general counsel concept is being eroded away, like the concept of the family doctor. Each problem confronted by a corporate legal department means shopping for the best-qualified lawyer at the most economical price. Tax matters may be sent to one firm, securities matters to another, and internal diligence checks to a third.

So getting business either from individuals or from corporations depends largely on the impressions you have made on others or on the reputation you have built for yourself.

Henry "Hank" Walter was a junior associate at Cravath, Swaine & Moore. One day he was assigned to work for client Kuhn Loeb on a routine oil exploration deal involving a ranch in Calgary. To his astonishment, he found himself face to face with the Duke of Windsor—the former King Edward VIII—who had abdicated to marry Wallis Simpson. The ranch was owned by the duke. Although the exploration resulted only in dry holes, the duke expressed his admiration for the young associate's work.

Later Hank left Cravath to start his own firm. His partners were Hugh Fulton, former counsel to the wartime Truman Committee (war contracts investigation) and Rudolph Halley, former counsel to the Kefauver Committee (mafia investigation). Sadly, Fulton, who weighed over three hundred pounds, soon died of a heart attack, and Halley died of cancer.

But miracle of miracles—the Duke of Windsor suddenly appeared from the past, said he remembered young Hank Walter, and became one of their first clients. He brought with him, as an independent client, his famous wife. The firm handled work on each of their autobiographies and on their other affairs in the United States.

Hank Walter says that he often played golf with the duke because during a golf game he could get the duke's attention. Otherwise, he said, the duke and duchess seemed to have been trained as royalty to have very short attention spans—about what was necessary for a sixty-second animated discussion in a receiving line. They treated their lawyers in the same fashion. The golf games, for which the duke always wore stylish plus fours, allowed Walter to find out critical details of the duke's legal problems. To induce the duke to play often enough to discuss important matters, Hank allowed the duke to drive off from the ladies' tees.

Another example: Chris Brady left an established firm in New York City to help found the five-man firm Hollyer, Jones, Pindyck, Brady & Chira. An early client for Chris was a partner from the firm Chris had just left. The partner had become involved in a personal lawsuit in which he was expected to be a witness; his own firm could not ethically handle the matter. He went straight to Chris because of his knowledge of how Chris had handled similar cases when he had been Chris's boss.

Similarly, sometimes a lawyer who has left a corporation, voluntarily or not, will get business from that corporation—or at least from his former co-workers. About a year ago, just after a hostile takeover, a lawyer in New York was fired summarily. He was bitter. He set up his own practice. The first client to come in his office door was a former officer of the same corporation; he had also been fired and now claimed to have been wrongfully deprived of a huge golden parachute. So the new sole practitioner is now gleefully suing his one-time tormentor, the raider that fired him, and is collecting legal fees, savoring the joy of revenge.

I mentioned Ralph C. Goldman earlier. Goldman set up his own firm in New York, a divorce practice. But his first client wasn't an angry spouse; he was Goldman's own dentist, who wanted Goldman to collect some unpaid bills for him.

Goldman accepted and started a lawsuit against a patient; he knew only her name and address. No answer was received, so he entered a default judgment and then wrote her that he could have her property seized.

A few days later there was a timid knock on the door of Goldman's office. He opened the door, and there stood a little old lady. She was five feet tall, weighed ninety pounds, was frail, and had white hair, eyes too old to sparkle but not too old to glisten, and a warm smile. She wore frayed clothes, but she was neat and proud, a lady; she looked like a beautiful young girl suddenly turned poor and old.

She said that she had received Goldman's letter, that she was on welfare, that she always tried to pay her bills on time, that she wanted to pay the dentist, but that she had not been able to manage out of her welfare check.

"I want to make amends to the dentist," she said. "I can't keep his work. I want you to take it back to him."

He started when the truth struck him: Her bill was for false teeth!

She placed a paper napkin daintily on his desk and reached toward her mouth. Goldman almost broke into tears.

"No! No!" he choked. "Let's see what we can do."

For two nights he couldn't sleep. What was he to do? What was he to say? He would have paid the bill himself, but he couldn't; this was his first case.

On the third day, his phone rang. A voice that he describes as the most "eloquent" he ever heard said, "My name is John E. Connelly, Jr. I represent a client who helps indigent women, and my client has heard of your case for the dentist. Can we pay you something and settle the case?"

Goldman was off like a shot. He called the dentist and offered to give up half his legal fee. The dentist would forgive half the bill. Connelly's client would pay half. All was agreed; it was done. The judgment against the little old lady was marked "satisfied."

Connelly was impressed by Goldman's fast action and by his tender concern. Connelly had numerous friends—mostly wealthy socialites among whom expensive divorces were commonplace. Often both the husband and the wife were his personal friends, and he didn't want to side with either. So he sent Goldman a flood of divorce cases among the wealthy. Goldman's first fee was $85,000—more than he had previously earned in his whole life.

So one of New York's most glittering divorce practices was born from a little old lady's false teeth.

What became of the little old lady? For years, every Christmas she left a handwritten note on plain paper under Goldman's office door. He never saw her. When the Christmas notes stopped, he knew she was dead.

A more cheerful start-up story is that of John V. A. "Van" Murray and Emile W. Jacques, who formed their own firm in Greenwich, Connecticut. Murray says, "We sat around all the time wondering how we could get business and how to market ourselves. So far, over 80 percent of our business has come through satisfied clients, who recommend us to others.

"But now," says Murray, "we are trying to develop a specialty business in condominiums so we can openly market that specialty."

To develop this specialty, Murray purchased a unit in each of several condominium developments around Greenwich and got himself elected to the board of directors of each. He then managed to become general counsel for every one of these developments.

He noted that under Connecticut law a condominium can form a tax district within itself. For example, if the overhead budget for an entire condominium was $100,000, perhaps $60,000 of this would be related to recreational areas, roads, police protection, and the like. Normally these would be paid for by a governmental unit. In order to make these deductible for federal income tax purposes, Murray set up a tax district and had the condominium residents pay $60,000 in "taxes" to the district and only $40,000 to the condominium itself for the rest of its budget. This created a significant tax deduction for the well-to-do unit owners.

Business is booming. When asked whether there was any financial sacrifice in starting the new firm, Murray smiles and says shyly, "We doubled our income in the first year and doubled it again in the second."

Sometimes a good reputation in one field can lead a practitioner into another field. A well-known wealthy Texan was referred to a start-up firm in New York to handle a minor local question. While he was in New York, he planned to visit one of New York's large factory-type firms to arrange the sale of some huge oil properties. He went first to the start-up firm, where he was so impressed by its hustle and quickness that he impetuously gave it the oil deal, too. He became such a large client that the small newcomer can now no longer be called that. It has become too solid and too big.

I mentioned earlier that entertaining prospects probably isn't a good way to get clients. Although in Hollywood movies it may be effective, in real life it can be downright dangerous.

A restaurant, a theater, a ball game, and the like can help cement personal relationships and usually do no harm. But these can create problems, too. Sometimes spouses don't get along. Sometimes, if you entertain two clients at once, the clients don't get along.

Entertaining may not be your cup of tea. Some lawyers who are tremendously impressive in a business context, an office conference, or a merger negotiation are boors or yokels in expensive restaurants. They can destroy a valuable image in one dinner party. They are better off avoiding entertainment.

In addition there are some things that in my younger days were regarded as entertainment but that no longer are; or maybe my crowd has gotten older. I am referring to "Big-Time Charlie" entertainment—Las Vegas, booze, and broads. Today one occasionally hears of "men of the evening" as well as "ladies of the evening."

Stay away! At craps or roulette, your prospective client may lose a large sum; at the other activities, worse can happen. One young lawyer friend of mine who was just starting out took a prospective client on such an evening. The result?

The prospect got a social disease but he didn't know it. The prospect's wife shortly got the same social disease and knew very well from whom. The wife got a divorce, their home, and their children. Before he was cured, the prospect got a tacit quarantine by his fellow workers, a brand-new one-room apartment, and a judgment to pay alimony for the rest of his life.

The lawyer? Forget it.

◆◆◆◆◆◆◆

Like any other business, a successful law practice depends on customers purchasing what you are offering—legal advice and counsel. You may be surprised to find that some of your first clients come to *you*, rather than your beating the bushes for *them*.

Keep in mind that clients need you—often even more than you need them. Particularly in the beginning you'll have to become something of an amateur psychologist to determine what your clients really want, both from you and from the other party or parties in the situation under discussion.

The only certainty in the practice of law is the inevitability of uncertainty. Business will come, but there's no way to predict how, when, or why. You may not be able to pick and choose your favorite legal specialty; chance, rather than planning, will often govern your first assignments. If that's the case, ride with the tide, go with the flow. Don't pretend to possess knowledge you don't have, but don't stress your ignorance, either. You can always dig up the essential information by yourself or with the aid of others.

Should you hire an advertising or public relations firm to make your name better known? Should you think in terms of marketing your services, even of utilizing give-aways or reduced fees for certain services?

You may think, in your innocent and idealistic heart, that such measures reduce the practice of law to the level of selling salad dressing or snake oil. But many firms have used these devices, often very successfully. Think it over; the times they are a-changing.

Somewhere in your legal career as an independent operator, politics is sure to raise its ugly—or, depending on your point of view, irresistible—head. Look over the political scene before you leap into it unawares. Are you a political animal? If so, do leap—but look carefully first.

Your clients may be slow in coming, and they may not be entirely to your liking. But they will come. Patience, perseverance, talent, and a little luck will send them your way.

3

WHERE TO
SET UP SHOP?

Where should you start out? Location will have a great impact on the practice and on the clients you'll be dealing with for years.

If you pick divorce law, your choice of location will be relatively open. But if you've decided on, say, corporate law, your choices of where to locate will be more limited.

At the turn of the century there was significant commercial law practice in Chicago, Milwaukee, Boston, and other cities, but New York City already had become the heart of big-time corporate practice. In the ensuing decades lawyers and the practice of law have become increasingly sophisticated outside New York, and many cities take on cases of great complexity. But Manhattan remains the undisputed champion in sheer size of corporate practice. There you will find megamergers, billion-dollar financings, and often major lawsuits.

Yet the New York metropolitan area, like other cities and their suburbs, also supports hundreds of small-town-type practices. Law firms in New York may consist of one person or several hundred.

There are 200,000 one-person firms in the country; probably one-fifth of them are in small towns. In the small towns of the rural South, the prairie states, and New England, practices tend to concentrate on human problems and are not directed as much toward institutions and financial dealings. Firms may contain five lawyers, or four, or one.

There is every kind of practice in between. Such cities as Raleigh, St. Louis, Denver, and San Diego offer rewarding opportunities; in size and complexity their practices are in the middle zone between those of the big cities and those of the small towns.

When I finished Harvard Law School, I went to work for Cravath, Swaine & Moore, then New York's largest firm. At that time they were heavily embroiled in the U.S. Justice Department's attempt to break up the Wall Street system of financing by syndications, which usually always included the same investment bankers. The case was monumental in commercial importance; the trial before Federal Judge Harold R. Medina lasted over a year. There were hundreds of lawyers, hundreds of witnesses, and hundreds of tons of documents; it was mammoth in size!

For me, it was a study in contrasts.

I asked for a three-month delay before starting at Cravath so I could work with my two uncles in the small town of Kinston, North Carolina, population 10,000. As Cravath pressed ahead with the monumental investment banking case, I was trying to recover a pig.

The creature had simply wandered away. The farmer who owned it had started the day intending to kill hogs but had decided that it was too hot and to hoe corn instead. In the process of his decision making he apparently left the pigpen open long enough for the pig to get out unnoticed. It headed for a neighbor's yard, where I believe it was eaten. In any event, although I tried, I never got any cooperation from the neighbor. I did not recover the pig.

The pig problem was a small case, fit to be delegated to a recent law school graduate. After a month's experience, I was entrusted with the larger assignment of recovering a bootlegger's car; it had been impounded by revenue agents who had caught our client after a good chase. I ultimately failed there, too.

My third case involved a client who had put up cash as bail money for his brother, who had been accused of theft. The brother had pleaded guilty, and the judge gave him a choice of thirty days in jail or a small fine. The prisoner had said that he preferred to pay the fine. Then he asked if he could go around the corner and borrow the funds from our client, his brother, and return immediately to pay the fine. The judge agreed.

The prisoner kept the first part of the bargain; he went around the corner. We never saw him after that.

The legal question now was whether the brother—our client—had forfeited the bail when the prisoner had appeared, pleaded guilty, been sentenced, and fled. Or had the bail merely guaranteed his appearance for trial, so that the later escape did not cause a forfeiture?

I told Uncle Fitzhugh, the attorney in the case, that I would research the matter.

"Don't bother, Harry, Jr.," he said, "unless you don't have anything else to do."

I didn't, so I looked into the law books. Suddenly I discovered that the state Supreme Court, its highest tribunal, had decided an identical case only the year before. The plaintiff, who had been in the same position as our client, had lost!

"Uncle Fitzhugh," I said, "we've lost. Here's a Supreme Court case just like ours, and it goes against us."

"Don't worry about that, Harry, Jr. Judge Sutton won't know anything about that decision, because he doesn't read them. Also, the Supreme Court has overruled him a lot recently, and he's mad and says he doesn't feel like following their rulings. Anyway, he likes to be fair rather than technical, like those people up there at Harvard. Let's drive over to Tarboro and have a drink with him and discuss it."

Disbelieving, I got in the car. We drove the thirty miles to Tarboro, went to Judge Sutton's hotel room with the local district attorney, had two or three stiff bourbons (or maybe white lightning, which Uncle Fitzhugh preferred). We talked about the tobacco crop and a local divorce case.

Then Uncle Fitzhugh said to the judge, "Jess, we've got that bail matter I called you about. I think it would be fair all around if we split it down the middle. The government can keep 50 percent and our man gets 50 percent back." The district attorney nodded.

"Fitzhugh," said Judge Sutton, "I think that's a good suggestion. It's a fair way all around. Tell the clerk to enter it that way."

We all shook hands.

In the next thirty-five years in New York I never resolved a matter that easily, on that friendly a basis, or, yes, on a fairer and squarer basis.

The settlement had nothing to do with the lawbooks; it contradicted them. But the judge was happy, the clerk was happy, Uncle Fitzhugh was happy, I was happy, and the client was happy. The client's brother, the prisoner, hasn't been seen anywhere near town to this day—or so his brother says. In New York, had the amounts been large enough, the same bail case could have consumed hundreds of lawyer hours.

Is that kind of practice too slow for you? Is the North Carolina life too quiet?

Steve Cowper, when he was a young lawyer, wanted politics and adventure. Where in the United States could you find both? How about Alaska?

After law school a friend told Steve of a job as assistant district attorney in Fairbanks, Alaska, which was then a small village. Steve drove there in his old jalopy and landed the job. Fairbanks is in the bush—the vast lands in northern and western Alaska populated mostly by the aboriginal Eskimos and Indians. At the time there were also bears, moose, and such to keep you on your toes. Steve spent a year in Vietnam as a reporter and then returned to Fairbanks to open his own law practice.

He was elected to the State House of Representatives but kept his active law practice, which was typical for most small towns—it handled personal injury cases, criminal defense, workers' compensation, and the like. A political report listed his 1985 income at $12,000. Even between politics and his law practice he still had time to be a marine research diver in southeastern Alaska in the summers. This avocation later led to his participation in the Smithsonian's live coral-reef tank exhibit at the Museum of Natural History in Washington, D.C.

As his own boss, he retained control of both his time and his destiny. Then, wearing cowboy boots and playing a five-string banjo, he campaigned for governor—successfully. He was inaugurated as Governor of Alaska on December 1, 1986.

How's that for career planning?

If Alaska is too cold for you but you want the outdoors, what about the legendary Old West? Anything can happen in a law practice there.

Tim Hasler graduated from Washington University Law School in St. Louis and shortly thereafter joined two other young lawyers in a new firm in Fort Collins, Colorado, which was then about 25,000 in population. Tim became a jack-of-all-trades. He handled real estate deals, houses, and ranches. In March and April he filled out tax returns for cowboys. All year round he did divorces. There also was litigation, which included a few mortgage foreclosures, evicting squatters, and some criminal cases that usually involved Saturday night brawls, jealous husbands, or occasionally thieves.

One day a "dude" walked in. He was Karl Schakel, from back East in Ohio. With Hasler's help Schakel bought a ranch; he fancied himself a cowboy. Hasler impressed Schakel. Later, happy on his ranch, Schakel became a broker to other dudes who wanted to play at being cowboys. Hasler handled the sales of ranches and sometimes the syndication of groups of buyers. He arranged the purchase of cattle, horses, and equipment and hired real cowboys to run the ranches for the dudes.

Then Schakel constructed farms that were irrigated with center pivots; each of them covered a quarter section, 160 acres. These were sold mainly to foreigners—Germans, French, Italians, Japanese, British—who wanted to invest in America and primarily in land, to protect against inflation and possible political instability in their own countries. Hasler worked for them and learned a good bit about international finance and banking in the process. Often the purchasers wanted a Texas corporation to hold the title for the ranches for various reasons, including a Nebraska law prohibiting alien ownership of land. Sometimes a Panamanian or a Netherland Antilles corporation to prevent people in the foreigners' home countries from tracing the title.

The farming business spread abroad. On a fee basis Schakel's company constructed irrigated farms in Morocco, Saudi Arabia, Kenya, Argentina, Paraguay, Egypt, Portugal, and Jamaica and gave advice to Zambia and the Dominican Republic. Hasler helped with these, preparing joint venture agreements and the like, and became an expert not only on the international aid programs of the United States and the United Nations but also on international trade in agricultural products.

It was a far cry from his early days as a small-town lawyer. Now Tim is an international financial and agricultural lawyer with three other lawyers in his office, still located in Fort Collins. Is there another law firm in all

Colorado, even in big-city Denver, that has international dealings of this variety? Probably not.

In Boston, Kathy O'Hara opened her own office there and waited for her first client. In he walked—a strange man about sixty-five years old.

He said that as a young lad of five in Dublin with his parents, he had been run over by a horse and dray and was pronounced dead on arrival at the hospital. He had revived only after a death certificate was filed. Now, sixty years later, his blood relatives in Dublin would not accept him as a family member; they believe he is an imposter because of the death certificate.

Kathy told me the problem but had not yet figured out what to do about it, so I do not know how this first client fared.

If you want to live in the New York area but have a small-town-type practice, you can.

Stephanie Lueders Rich was working for a large corporate law firm in New York City as a tax specialist, but she wanted a different type of practice. So she joined a small new law firm in a suburb.

Her first client was a far cry from any she had seen before. She was a beautiful woman prisoner who had been convicted, in a highly publicized case, of complicity in the stabbing of her husband by a delivery man during a drunken episode. The now-recovered husband was suing his imprisoned wife for damages. Rich went to the public library and read the tabloid accounts of the stabbing. Then in a flash of insight she countersued for libelous statements made to the press about the beautiful prisoner. She brought the husband's suit to a standoff and got a zero settlement from him. She came to like the unfortunate prisoner and now visits that lady in jail occasionally, taking her own three-year-old son with her.

A far cry from the world of corporate mergers and acquisitions?

The many differences between Wall Street, Main Street, the Wild West, and Alaska may affect your choice of location. New York, for example, attracts large numbers of lawyers with no family or personal connections nearby. But elsewhere your choice will probably be dictated as much by family or personal relationships as by the type of law you intend to practice.

One lawyer aspired to become an Olympic diver; so he opened a firm in Miami, where he could dive year round—which he did into his seventies.

Another attorney picked Houston solely because it was then predicted to be the fastest-growing legal center outside New York—a prediction that did not fully come true.

Absent these special considerations, you are likely to try to be near family or friends—either from childhood or from law school—and they will be of significant help to you in getting your new life in order and your law practice started. If you can prepare a will, you will be amazed at how many people your mother will tell that to. When things seem tough, a cousin can help keep your morale on an even keel. Classmates may work for potential clients and help open doors. Or perhaps you are lucky enough to be the youngest of thirteen children and have twelve older ones to tout you.

On virtually no occasion is a lawyer "summoned" to a particular town. Sometimes doctors are sought by a community that doesn't have a doctor; clergymen are often called to a church with no clergyman. Saloon women flocked to the Old West to fill a void; in a sense they, too, were called.

But I doubt that any place in this country lacks lawyers. It is true that poor people sometimes cannot get private legal services because they cannot pay at all, and they have to resort to public interest firms, legal aid, or social work. It is also true that people in middle-class areas complain that legal fees are too high; but in most cases they do pay those fees and suffer no real lack of legal services. In both instances—for the poor and the middle class—the problem is a lack not of lawyers near at hand but of the means of paying them. The rich, of course, have no such problems.

So you cannot pick the location of your new law firm by looking for a place that "needs" it. It's different from seeking a job as an employee. That's relatively easy; you go where the employer is.

Instead, choose a place, first, that has the kind of law practice you think you would enjoy and be good at—Wall Street or Main Street or in between—and, second, that is near your family and friends—or even your enemies, if you have earned their respect. If a skier finds a mountain nearby, a hunter finds a moose at hand, a diver finds the ocean nearby, or a cold-blooded lawyer finds the sunshine—that's okay, but these are pluses, not prime movers.

◆◆◆◆◆◆◆

If you decide to specialize, your choice of specialty will help determine where to start out. Divorces know no geographical bounds, but big-time corporate law is definitely centered in the big cities, particularly New York.

Generally, the biggest bucks are made in the biggest cities, but small towns have their attractions, too. There is an abundance of diversity, a certain hometown feeling, a great opportunity to become an integral part of a community in small towns.

Wall Street or Main Street? In all likelihood, your decision will depend more on personal inclination than on objective considerations. Your family, friends, old school chums, and colleagues in the legal profession can be of immense help to you when you're starting out.

Unlike doctors, lawyers are seldom "summoned" to a town or region where their services are needed. So it's your choice, and you'll be happiest if you select an area where you can practice the kind of law and lead the kind of life you like the most, where you can hunt or fish or attend the opera and ballet, if that's what you prefer and count on a little help from family or friends.

4

CHOOSING A PARTNER—OR GOING IT ALONE

Do you want a partner?

A friend of mine, Henry C. Neel, practiced alone for twenty years. Suddenly, without any warning whatsoever, at the peak of his successful career in Henderson, Kentucky, he simultaneously married a lovely woman and formed a new law firm—two new partnerships at once.

I didn't ask Henry about the marriage partnership; the benefits there were self-evident when one saw the bride (Henry had a good eye for that sort of thing), and he had had a harrowing life as a bachelor. I did ask him, however, to compare having law partners and practicing alone.

Henry said it was a trade-off; autonomy and control in exchange for administrative improvement and larger income.

"First," said Henry, "when I was a single practitioner, I spent a good deal of my own time tending to housekeeping, such as library matters, billing, accounts receivables, expenses, staff problems, and the like, and now the firm has relieved me of all of those chores. Of course," he added, "you might wind up with an angry secretary because the firm insists that she have an up-to-date word processor instead of the typewriter she loves.

"Sometimes the firm commandeers my secretary for other lawyers' work in an emergency, which infuriates me no end, although I recognize the necessity," he said after further thought.

"Also, when I was a lone practitioner," Henry continued, "I was a jack-of-all-trades, handling litigation, municipal bonds, utilities rate-setting, estates, divorces—everything. It was fun.

"I chose the cases I worked on—those that I liked best. If I represented an attractive woman in a divorce, I could elect to devote more time to that than if I just represented the poor husband—at least, before I got married I could. If I wanted to take the day off, I did. Now, as a partner, I'm slotted into a specialty, whether I want it or not. I have a reputation for being able to handle difficult litigation, and it all devolves on me. There are more pressure points, and I have to work harder. I have to stay in the office regular hours. The trade-off here is more money. My earnings have increased substantially."

Henry said a lot in that brief telephone chat; partners can be a big help. And there are other advantages that Henry didn't mention. Let's list some.

A partner may be a good *substitute*. If you have to be in court or out of town or sick, your partner can act as "hand holder" for your clients until you get back. Probably half or more of the problems that excite clients will go away by themselves, but until then the client wants to talk to a lawyer in a hurry. And he or she might go to a competitor if your partner isn't there to listen. A good enough partner could even become a full-fledged back-up—say, during your long vacations.

A partner is also valuable as a *co-worker*. If you have an offer to settle a case, should you accept the offer or go for broke? The client may be too emotional to discuss it with you. Another lawyer with a fresh look can be a great help as a sounding board. Sometimes he or she can even do some of your work, either alone or jointly with you.

A partner can also be a *specialist*, saving you the time and work of learning the field of law he or she already knows. You can specialize in something different from your partner's specialty. In older firms, taxes and "blue sky" work usually are specialties. In a smaller firm, divorce might be one, or real estate, or criminal law.

A partner often serves as a good *promotion piece*. If someone at the country club has a problem with their maid's immigration status, you might suddenly remember that your partner is an expert—a fact that had not previously occurred to you. Of course, be sure to warn your partner about what you've done, so he or she can prepare. It's hard to claim that you yourself are an expert if you're not; that may be discounted as bragging or someone may put you to the test, with resulting embarrassment.

Your partner also may be a born *"rainmaker"* and generate more business than he or she can handle alone. A true partner, not just an office sharer, will help keep you busy until you have built up your own following of clients.

A partner can also be a *synergist* in that your combined well-being probably will be greater than the sum of the parts. A partner can strengthen morale in difficult times and can add financial strength in the capital supplied to the firm. A partner also spreads the risk of business slowdowns; the partner's business may surge when yours is slack. Services can be shared.

Especially, if there is an age disparity, one partner may serve the other as a *buyer or seller* of the business. That is, the older does less work gradually as he turns it over to the younger, and the younger works harder as a way of paying the older for this business. Although partnership agreements do not state this openly, they bring about this result in practice.

All this sounds great! But remember, my friend Henry Neel told me that having partners is a trade-off. I asked him for an explanation.

"Having partners means having meetings," according to Henry. "Meetings are a disease of partners. Sometimes I can't take calls from clients because I'm in a meeting with my partners. I hear that only charity ball committees have more meetings—or maybe people in Hollywood.

"We have committees, too," he said. "Committees mean more meetings. I believe we could get along with two fewer partners if we didn't have all those meetings."

Henry's words struck a responsive chord in me. Partnership meetings! It seems to me that I have been in them for thousands of hours. One forty-five-minute meeting can seem to last several hours.

My firm, Olwine, runs along pretty well by itself—much better when it is left alone than when twenty partners try to manage it collectively. Twenty lawyers deciding a nonlegal problem! Normally Olwine has no real business to conduct at its biweekly partners' meeting. But with so many lawyers present, anything can become a major agenda item.

For example, if someone says that the flowers on the reception desk are nice, a litigator immediately takes issue as to their color or odor. Another brings up human allergies, which mean environmental problems.

The litigators feed on each other. Why not potted plants instead of cut flowers? Or glass flowers—they would be even cheaper! The daily expense of the flowers is debated in a vacuum since no one knows their cost.

Do we want a bright flashy lobby or shabby gentility? The oratory grows more extravagant until the tax lawyers, accustomed to placing all things in neat categories, no longer recognize the topic or remember the issue. The corporate lawyers, accustomed to the meticulous precision of a bond indenture, for no apparent reason try to identify the flowers by species, although they do not know the names of any of them. The consideration of this vital issue is never concluded. Debate stops only when the litigators and corporate lawyers, or some of them, have to seek relief of another kind in the partners' loo. I know how Henry feels about partnership meetings.

Until the second half of the 19th century, the decision of having a partner or going it alone was not necessarily important. Even New York firms usually did not consist of more than two lawyers, and it was easy to discard one if things weren't working out.

In earlier days many great men practiced alone, or virtually so. The long list of sole practitioners includes Alexander Hamilton, Chancellor James Kent, and John Jay—and don't forget Daniel Webster.

Greatness does not require a partner. But office sharing and client sharing were common in earlier days; those arrangements began to evolve into true partnerships in the latter half of the nineteenth century.

And the firms at that time were small, even as tiny as your new firm is apt to be.

Hubbell's 1871 directory of New York firms, the earliest extant issue of the present-day Martindale-Hubbell Law Directory, lists the following firms as recommended by two banks or two leading merchants.

NUMBER OF PARTNERS	NAME
5	Evarts, Southmayd & Choate [Joseph H. Choate was one of the great trial lawyers and ambassador to Great Britain]
4	Lord, Day & Lord

Also in New York at that time were the following firms that did not appear in Hubbell's lists in 1871 or 1872 (perhaps for not seeking the required recommendations). They made their first appearance in the 1873 edition of Hubbell's.

NUMBER OF PARTNERS	NAME
—	Alexander & Green
4	Arthur, Phelps & Knevals [one partner was Chester A. Arthur, later U.S. President]
2	Carter & Russell
2	Compton & Root [one partner was Elihu Root, later Secretary of War, Secretary of State, and U.S. Senator]

No other firms existed that are familiar today.

The Carter listed above in Carter & Russell was Walter S. Carter, about whom Otto E. Koegel wrote a fascinating biography, *Walter S. Carter, Collector of Young Masters.* Carter came to New York in 1871 and had a profound impact on legal partnerships as we now know them and as you will encounter them. He arrived after the great Chicago fire as legal representative of the Chicago creditors of fifteen suspended fire insurance companies. He opened the office of Carter & Russell.

There Carter originated the now-common practice of seeking one or more of the best graduates of the leading law schools each year and training them through clerkships in his office. After that they either became partners or left to form their own firms or to join others. "Carter's Kids" became recognized as the best and brightest young lawyers of their time. They remained long enough to insure that there were always experienced ones in the office but not long enough to lose their ambition to rise above the position of law clerk.

Carter usually had only one or two partners at a time, but there was a constant turnover of his partners.

"Carter's Kids"—partners and law clerks—became the foundation of many of today's blue-chip firms in New York. They became founding partners or "name" partners in the following offshoots of the Carter firm.

Satterlee & Stephens
Cravath, Swaine & Moore
Wilkie, Farr & Gallagher
Mitchell, Capron, Marsh, Angulo & Cooney
Jackson & Nash
Cadwalader, Wickersham & Taft
Mudge, Rose, Guthrie, Alexander & Ferdon
Rogers & Wells
Hughes, Hubbard & Reed

In addition, former partners and associates of the Carter firms and successors and split-offs became leading partners in

Carter, Ledyard & Milburn
Donovan, Leisure, Newton & Irvine
Delafield, Hope & Linker
Milbank, Tweed, Hadley & McCoy
Shearman & Sterling
Breed, Abbott & Morgan

About three decades after the early Hubbell's listings and Carter's arrival in New York, reflecting in no small part other firms' emulation of Carter in selecting partners for excellence, Hubbell's Legal Directory for the year 1900 listed the following as the largest firms in New York City.

NUMBER OF PARTNERS	NAME
9	Carter, Hughes and Dwight
9	Davis, Stone & Auerbach
6	Reed, Simpson, Thacher & Barnum [now Simpson, Thacher & Bartlett]
6	Stetson, Jennings & Russell [now Davis, Polk, Wardwell]
5	Sullivan & Cromwell

NUMBER OF PARTNERS	NAME
4	Seward, Gutherie & Steele [now Cravath, Swaine & Moore]
4	Strong & Cadwalader [now Cadwalader, Wickersham & Taft]
4	Root, Howard, Winthrop & Stimson [now Winthrop, Stimson, Putnam & Roberts]
3	Shearman & Sterling

Your own new firm might start out as small as most of those were at the turn of the century. Today some of these organizations are the huge powerhouses of Wall Street. Maybe your new firm can evolve the same way. But that depends in good part on what you want, on what kind of partners you pick, and on how you organize your firm.

Carter's system was modified substantially by the great Paul D. Cravath, who was at one time a partner with Carter and Charles Evans Hughes in the tiny firm known as Carter, Hughes & Cravath. Cravath subscribed to Carter's approach—"the brightest kids up or out"—but he added the elements of specialization and organization. He recognized that a law firm could attain the best results for big clients only if it could provide specialists in the various fields that were daily becoming more important and vastly complicated—securities, taxes, reorganizations, and trusts.

Before Cravath's time, there had been little attempt at the scientific organization of law offices. In most, each partner worked with his own assistants for a particular client. Back when firms were small—less than ten partners—Cravath transformed the system into a team approach. Lawyers with broad general experience worked closely with specialists who had received highly concentrated training.

Today there are many partners in such firms. Perhaps 30 firms nationwide have 100 or more partners. There are 307—count them, 307—with Baker, McKenzie. Some firms are gigantic; there are 800 lawyers, including associates, at Baker, McKenzie (which reports 12,500 active clients). There are 700-odd lawyers at Skadden, Arps and Jones, Day, and 500-odd or 400-odd at 6 other firms. (The above does not imply that *all* lawyers are "odd," although quite a few qualify.)

Conversely there are perhaps 200,000 one-person law firms, and there is everything in between. So you have lots of choices.

If you decide you want a partner, what kind of person should you choose? Walter S. Carter picked the most brilliant "kids" he could find. When their importance within the firm began to approach his, they moved on—or were pushed out—to start their own firms. Only Charles Evans Hughes, his son-in-law, remained. One associate of the Carter firm, Lindsay Russell, left the firm in 1902 and later wrote,

> To give an idea of the deep water I was in and how far outclassed, this firm had in its membership Hughes, later Chief Justice, Dwight, nephew of the president of Yale, Schurman, brother of the president of Cornell, Colby Chester, later president of General Foods, and several other honor men from Yale and Harvard. . . .
>
> [Carter] picked his partners as Connie Mack picked ball players, usually dropping them when they demanded or earned as much as he did.

Perhaps your practice doesn't require the brilliance Carter sought. Maybe patience, perseverance, consistency, and equilibrium are more important in your context.

Possibly your partner has already been selected for you by being a family member. There are many father-son and brother-brother partnerships. I know also of husband-wife partnerships, father-daughter partnerships, a mother-son partnership, and a partnership of twin sisters. I haven't run across a mother-daughter or sister-brother partnership; these will come.

I dealt with a firm in Santo Domingo named Troncoso & Caceres that has eight male partners. All of them are closely related by blood or marriage to the others—except Luis Mora Guzman, who was introduced to me as an outsider admitted only for his ability.

Generally, family partnerships are fine. Occasionally they aren't. One lawyer in Newark told me that he had practiced with his older brother for five years. "It was hell. I was a go-go young lawyer. I wanted to expand, grow, market ourselves, go first class. My brother was satisfied, complacent, security minded. It became antagonistic. It was worse than a bad marriage, because you can get away from a fussing spouse in the mornings. Finally one day I told my brother I was leaving. He never forgave me. He still keeps my name on the partnership sign, even though I've asked him to take it off. He doesn't want his friends to know I left him, but they all know it already. I told them."

Doreen Weisfuse of the New York husband-wife firm of Weisfuse & Weisfuse says, "There are great advantages in a husband-wife partnership. First, we don't argue about which partner makes what percentage of the firm income; it all goes into our family pot. Second, we don't argue about whose name comes first in the firm's name; we each claim to be first. Third, this arrangement enables me to practice real estate law from our home in Scarsdale, where we have two boys ages three and six. I communicate by computer or telephone with the New York office, where my husband Marty does medical malpractice work, and I go there maybe once a week. I can meet the family demands and practice law, too."

Do they ever argue? "Not over the law practice," says Doreen.

What do you name a husband-wife partnership? Doreen Weisfuse and her husband elected to use both their names, since they didn't have to decide whose name was first. Raoul Felder, who is known in New York as "Captain Divorce," made a different decision. His partnership with his wife Myrna is known by the authoritative corporate title, "The Firm of Raoul Lionel Felder, P.C."

In another husband-wife "partnership" the wife, who is not a member of the bar, had been working on immigration matters as a paralegal for a law firm in New York. Her husband was a lawyer employed on the legal staff of a corporation. Suddenly it occurred to the woman that she was doing the same work at the firm as lawyers but was being paid less. After a conference with her husband, he hung out a shingle on their house in the suburbs, and she went to work for him as an unsalaried paralegal.

Now he continues to go to work each day for the corporation in the city, and she operates the office at their home. When the lawyer husband arrives home at night, he reviews the papers from her day's practice and signs letters that she has already written for his signature. It takes about fifteen minutes each day. This woman, not a lawyer herself, has built a flourishing legal business in their home in immigration matters. The net income from that business is now in excess of the husband's salary.

"She does all the work, and he takes all the credit," said an admiring golf companion of the husband. She smiles at such remarks because she opens the mail containing the fees and thus controls the purse strings.

As for sister-sister partnerships, consider the identical twins in the Detroit firm of Lloyd & Lloyd. Their father, Leon, named them after himself; they are Leona Loretta Lloyd and Leonia Janetta Lloyd. Their names sound alike, and they look exactly alike. One newspaper said they also talk alike and walk alike.

Leona says, "Clients are satisfied as long as they're talking to one of us."

That may be an understatement; the twins were models

before they became lawyers. They specialize in entertainment law and represent several well-known pop artists. They see no need for another partner. Things are just fine all in the family.

If you select a partner from outside your family, don't be surprised to find that lots of lawyers have unpleasant personalities. Often they are harmless, and you eventually find out that the angry look or the growling voice is simply an inborn characteristic of the person and does not indicate hostility. You can learn to live with such a lawyer as a partner, once you understand him or her.

Unfortunately, there are others who never become bearable. These include types who think that they are in competition with their partners; they imagine that the way to win the competition is to constantly put their partners down, either through confrontations or by belittling their achievements. Or there are types who feel that they have to be the boss and who cannot share decision making. You should avoid partners of these types.

Despite his fabulous insight into human nature, even Walter S. Carter occasionally made mistakes and selected men with uncurable bad traits. He wrote Charles Evans Hughes in 1892 about one such partner, George M. Pinney.

The same roof cannot hold Pinney and the rest of the office; this, I think I may say, without a single exception. He has no business in any firm of which he is not the controlling power; he is another of those fellows who sighs for liberty—liberty not only to do as he pleases, but to have everyone else do as he pleases, and if there is one way more peculiarly exasperating and offensive than another, he will be sure to adopt it. I don't blame him a particle, he was made so. If you knew the Pinney stock as I know it, you would not be surprised, and with all this, he has got an exceedingly warm and generous side; many essential merits, and very great ability.

Carter was neither the first to find fault with a partner nor the last. Melvin Belli, the "king of torts," defended Jack Ruby, the killer of Lee Harvey Oswald. He is said to have changed the locks on the office door of his partner, Vasilios Choirlos. He engaged in lawsuits against Choirlos, as well as his own former managing attorney and several other lawyers from his firm. One lawyer noted that Belli, who wears purple boots and once posed with a human skeleton in a convertible automobile, had had five wives; he had ousted his lawyers like his wives, or vice versa, according to this lawyer. Belli, who has represented such clients as Mae West and Martha Mitchell, says of his former law associates, "Thank God they're gone."

Edward Bennett Williams has represented the greatest collection of celebrities of all time—unless Howe & Hummell, at the turn of the century, has the edge. Williams has represented Adam Clayton Powell, the famed Harlem congressman, on tax fraud charges; Senator Joe McCarthy; former Treasury Secretary John Connally; labor boss Jimmy Hoffa; and oilman Marvin Davis.

Yet with all this legal business, he had a number of disagreements with his partner, Nicholas Chase. It is said that Chase wanted to take cases where "justice" was on his side, while Williams was more prone to take on any good exciting fight, such as the Adam Clayton Powell tax fraud case (where Powell's secretary had a faulty memory) and Jimmy Hoffa's trial for bribery (where boxing champion Joe Louis appeared in the courtroom and hugged Hoffa before the jurors, many of whom were black). Chase left the partnership to seek cases more to his liking.

Peter Megaree Brown, a longtime friend of mine, left Cadwalader, Wickersham & Taft after 26 years and formed a two-man partnership with Whitney North Seymour, Jr., who had left Simpson, Thacher & Bartlett after 33 years.

Two senior partners left two prestigious law firms.

Why? They wanted a firm in the "barrister" or "counselor at law" tradition; they wanted direct personal contact with clients at all times.

In 1983 Brown wrote an article that appeared in both *The International Herald Tribune* and *The New York Times* in which he referred to "the flood of new lawyers . . . one lawyer for every 388 people. . . . Two-thirds of all lawyers are in the United States. . . . The pyramiding monster, multistate and multinational law firms, whose dehumanizing bureaucracies chill professional independence."

On a more personal level, Brown said of his severance from Cadwalader that, before leaving, "I learned that I was no longer head of litigation when I got an envelope, and I learned that I was no longer chairman of the Ethics Committee when I got another envelope."

This traumatic experience with envelopes may have led him to think of the rising "incivility" in law firms and to lead off his article with this sentence: "The American legal profession is declining."

As a precaution in their new partnership, Brown and Seymour do not share fees. They keep separate books, make separate profits, and have separate bank accounts. Their affairs are not commingled. Peter Brown will never get another letter in a sealed envelope with news of a demotion or a change in responsibilities.

Sometimes partners are gotten rid of in wholesale lots. In New York, John Russell of Hale, Russell and about twenty other lawyers left that forty-man law firm and joined Winthrop Stimson, leaving 50 percent of the Hale, Russell lawyers behind, some with no apparent livelihood.

Gordon Spivak and seventeen other lawyers left Lord, Day & Lord with $6 million worth of cases and went to Coudert Brothers. The issue had been who would pick new partners.

At the Newport Beach firm of Kray, Newsmeyer the

senior partner, Steven Kray, tried to get three new partners to sign the firm's loan documents. He had difficulty with them, so he announced that he was becoming a partner at Finley, Kumble and taking the three with him in the reduced status of associates; they would no longer be partners.

Finley, Kumble, in fact, has been involved in so many such deals that, as *The American Lawyer* said, "We have seen one man—Marshall Manley of Finley, Kumble—develop as the Carl Icahn of partner-raiders, luring dozens of malcontents to his firm with promises of more money."

Finley, Kumble, with 200 partners and more than 600 lawyers, has obtained many or most of its partners through such deals. But they have not been immune to the trauma of partners going in the other direction; they have lost or ousted many partners along the way to the tune of much accompanying litigation.

Sometimes, despite drawbacks of one sort or another, a partnership puts up with a partner who causes it trouble. Often this occurs when the troublemaking partner happens also to be a "rainmaker"—a big business-getter.

Take the late Roy M. Cohn, former assistant to Senator Joseph McCarthy in the Army-McCarthy hearings and the assistant prosecutor in the Rosenberg spy case. He was accused repeatedly of professional misbehavior, including mishandling clients' funds and tampering with jurors; the bar's disciplinary committee recommended disbarment. He was tried on criminal charges and acquitted; finally he was disbarred in 1986, shortly before his death.

Controversies over Cohn lasted through much of his partnership with Thomas A. Bolan of Saxe, Bacon & Bolan, P.C. Despite the accusations, there always was a considerable demand for Cohn's services, even though he often didn't provide them himself but delegated them, seemingly almost casually. So he was considered a valuable partner if a troublesome one; Bolan defended him constantly.

Another aspect of Cohn's partnership arrangement was unique: as Cohn himself acknowledged, for years he was bankrupt. My own law firm, representing Lionel Corporation, won a very sizable judgment against Cohn personally, arising out of earlier business ventures; but the judgment was neither collected nor collectible.

Many other creditors chased Cohn as well; none collected, to my knowledge. Cohn had no assets and often said so. How did he survive? Well, all his "possessions" subject to attachment actually belonged to the law firm. His apartment, his limousine, his furniture—all his daily bills were paid by the law firm—even his meals, haircuts, manicures, and entertainment. Meanwhile Cohn lived in a world of glitter and hobnobbed with the likes of Francis Cardinal Spellman, Terence Cardinal Cooke, William F. Buckley, Barbara Walters, William Safire, countless judges and politicians, and luminaries of the theatrical and television worlds. Cohn had no possessions—and no expenses!

No one could touch him except the bar and the courts—and eventually the Grim Reaper. His creditors—or his enemies, as he probably regarded them—were powerless against him. What other law firm has had such an arrangement with a partner? Not even Finley, Kumble offers such a secure arrangement to its recruits.

You might be asking yourself at this point, "Can anything else go wrong involving my partner?" Yes, it can.

At Simpson, Thacher & Bartlett a "rainmaking" partner, Joel Dolkart, age sixty-two, stole $1.5 million in fees paid his firm by its client Gulf +Western and another $1 million from his previous law firm.

At Shea & Gould, a rising associate, Peter P. Smith III, not yet a partner, stole $70,000 of the fees paid his firm by Bethlehem Fabricators.

At Finley, Kumble a former "name" partner, Robert Persky, was convicted of securities fraud and served a term in prison.

At Wachtell, Lipton partner Ilan Reich pleaded guilty to using insider information in the securities scandal involving Ivan Boesky and was sentenced to a year in prison.

At Donovan, Leisure a brilliant, hard-working lawyer with an impeccable reputation, Mahlon Perkins, inexplicably withheld documentary evidence in the *Berkey Photo* v. *Kodak* case and falsely said he had destroyed it, probably contributing to a jury award of $113 million to Berkey and causing Kodak to switch its legal defense from Donovan, Leisure to Sullivan & Cromwell. That incident led to public doubts about Donovan, Leisure's very survival. Of its 190 lawyers at the time of the incident, about seventy were lost, including almost a third of its partners. It was a horrendous downward slide.

In other firms partners have simply cracked up psychologically, suddenly trying to jump out a window, cowering under a desk, throwing a chair at a secretary. Maybe the problems are overwork, pressing debts, or an unexplained loss of confidence; maybe they're innate. In any event the other partner or partners may be suddenly left without the services of an incapacitated colleague—and perhaps with the burden of caring for him or her.

Fortunately, only a minority of the partners in the legal world become burdens to their colleagues. Most are able, decent men and women with whom you would be happy to practice. Some are super. Just imagine yourself helping to form the firm of Carter, Hughes & Cravath—Walter S. Carter, Charles Evans Hughes, Paul D. Cravath, and you. You would have been, or should have been, awed when you looked at yourself in the mirror while shaving or powdering your nose.

In a majority of partnerships there is a great deal of mutual respect and, perhaps more important, a strong feeling of mutual responsibility toward each other. Most partners have a conscience and a sense of decency and loyalty.

With the right partners—those with a conscience and sense of decency—a partnership often makes more sense than a solitary practice. It enables you to offer specialization; it provides back-up in rush times; it spreads the risks; it adds financial strength; it strengthens morale in difficult times; it is easier to "sell" to prospective clients.

I called my friend Henry Neel in Henderson, Kentucky, to see how his new partnership was going. When he picked up the phone, I asked him about the firm.

"It's fine," he said. "My partners are great guys. Everyone pitches in. When I'm too busy, someone else is there to help. Business is good; income is up. It's terrific to have partners."

"That's great," I said. "Now I want to talk to you about maybe coming out for the Kentucky Derby."

"Fine, fine," Henry said, suddenly sounding rushed. "But I'll have to call you later about that—as soon as I can. I can't talk anymore right now. One of my damned partners has called a partnership meeting."

◆◆◆◆◆◆◆

Are partners necessary? Of course not. Can they be helpful? Of course.

Which is more important to you—complete autonomy and control, or administrative benefits and the chance to earn more money?

The partnerships so common today were virtually unknown a century ago, although office sharing and client sharing began to evolve into full-fledged partnerships toward the end of the nineteenth century.

Today, some giant firms contain as many as one hundred or more partners. You're more likely to start off with one or two.

If you decide to have partners, what should you look for?

Decide for yourself. Maybe it's brilliance and perspicacity. Or perhaps organizational ability and dependability are more important. You may want a partner whose specialty complements, rather than duplicates, your own. If you're not good at drumming up clients, you may want to seek a "rainmaker," a person who seemingly without effort attracts clients by the carload.

So if you're truly independent and want to make all decisions yourself, go it alone. But well-chosen partners, with the proper combination of ability, personality, and decency, can add legal and financial strength, spread your risks, and enable you to offer many more services than a one-person shop.

5

HOW MUCH TO CHARGE

As a boy I often went to family gatherings at Uncle John's. For the adults he would produce bottles of differing shapes, none with labels—Mason jars, vinegar jugs—and all filled with an almost-clear liquid. Glasses and ice would appear. Drinks were poured. A powerful, somewhat repellent, but very familiar odor filled the room, heavy like a wet fog. It was moonshine, white lightning—the best. Uncle John was known for serving only the best in moonshine; estimates of its proof were frightening.

Uncle John had a whole cellar full of it.

Uncle John was not a moonshiner or a bootlegger. He was a lawyer. He had probably the biggest and best clientele in the county because of his reputation for success at everything he tried—politics, law, business. And in that county some of the finest clients had only one medium of exchange—white lightning, which they made themselves in the woods, risking their lives beside their copper tubing and pots. The potion they produced smelled to high heaven, but it tasted like heaven and was equally explosive inside you and when lighted with a match. So when a client couldn't pay money, Uncle John would perform the client's legal work and take his fee in moonshine, if it was good moonshine.

At family gatherings the mood of our group would change spontaneously. Recollections were exchanged, cousins threw their arms around each other, and glasses were refilled. Uncle John said, "Normally, I don't take a second drink, but . . . "

My grandfather had been a small-town medical doctor in the same community before the turn of the century. Many people who came to see him were truly ill. They had to come, but they couldn't pay money. So they brought chickens, vegetables, pigs, geese, rabbits, or wild game—whatever they could. Moonshine was like gold, except that my grandfather didn't drink alcohol and had to give it away—or sell it, before Prohibition.

My lawyer uncle of the next generation, Uncle John, wouldn't take his fees in chickens, vegetables, pigs, and such. Moonshine, however, was maybe better than money, just as it had been in my grandfather's time. Unlike my grandfather, my uncle and his contemporaries neither gave it away nor sold it. They drank it, with friends, with clients, with judges. They drank it after court, at funerals, at weddings, on Saturdays, sometimes before court, in motels, at home, in the next town, in the state capital, wherever the law took them.

Moonshine, unfortunately, is no longer good for paying bills. Brand-name liquors are readily available now. Lawyers want cash, and so do their spouses.

So how much can you charge your clients in cash?

Before you answer that question, ask yourself several others: Will the client get mad and go to another lawyer next time? Will you get a reputation for overcharging? Or of being so cheap that something must be wrong? Can you meet your overhead?

A recent survey published in the magazine *Of Coun-*

sel contained the following typical billing rates for established firms.

LOCATION	CHARGE PER HOUR FOR TOP PARTNER	CHARGE PER HOUR FOR BOTTOM ASSOCIATE
Atlanta	$200	$55
Boston	220	60
Chicago	180	60
Denver	165	60
Houston	210	70
Los Angeles	225	70
New York	260	75
San Francisco	200	60
Washington, D.C.	200	60

By contrast, a partner in Richmond or St. Louis might charge $100 an hour, an associate $40. In small towns there is very often no fixed hourly rate. Each case is billed according to the client's ability (and willingness) to pay and according to the success of the effort, or lack of it.

"All well and good," you think. "But what do those numbers mean to *me*? I'm just starting out."

Well, to analyze that, we might start with the fact that there are about 450,000 practicing lawyers (apart from another 300,000 practicing things other than law); they gross about $35 billion each year, perhaps more.

That's $70,000 per practicing lawyer in fees nationwide. And it probably means approximately $35,000 in average take-home pay, after shelling out for rent, secretary, and other expenses.

But those are average figures. The biggest firm in the country in terms of fees is Skadden, Arps in New York, with about $225 million per year. That amounts to over $1.6 million per partner, or nearly $320,000 per lawyer, including associates. This combination gives partners take-home pay averaging more than $500,000; the top partners receive well over $1 million a year. (A partner in firms with many associates makes a profit on the associates, so the partner's take-home pay is often more than he charges for his own time.)

To put this in perspective, compare the fees of Walter S. Carter before the turn of the century. In an insurance case involving the great Chicago fire, he obtained an 80 percent settlement. His services extended over three and a half years and included ten hearings before the referee. In 1876 his fee was $1,000.

Other Carter firm bills were three-dollar fees for each of two meetings with a partner in 1877 and twenty-five dollars a day for two days of a partner's time in 1878.

A young lawyer at that time was happy to make $137 for nine months' work. In 1893 *The American Commonwealth* reported that the largest annual income of any American law firm was believed to be $250,000.

What happened? Why have legal fees escalated from Carter's $1,000 in the 1870s to Skadden, Arps's $225 million in 1986?

Murray Teigh Bloom, in his 1968 book *The Trouble With Lawyers*, tracks the history of total legal fees nationally from $1.3 billion in 1950 to $2 billion in 1955 and $4 billion in 1966. Now, long after that book was published, it is up to a staggering $35 billion a year.

Increases in the number of Americans and American industries account for a lot of this growth. But the "fixing" of legal fees by bar associations was a major contributor until 1975. More than half the states adhered to statewide schedules of minimum fees set by these associations, and about eight hundred local bar groups had similar schedules. At that time, the American Bar Association Committee on Professional Ethics Opinion 302 stipulated that

> The habitual charging of fees less than those established by a minimum fee schedule, or the charging of such fees

without proper justification, may be evidence of unethical conduct.

Most, but not all, lawyers welcomed minimum fee schedules. They eliminated bargaining with clients and clients' "shopping" for the cheapest fees.

Some lawyers opposed set fees on principle. Others were unaffected. Among them were probate lawyers, whose charges were usually based on a percentage of the estate, not on time worked or on difficulties encountered. And the probate judges saw that their fees were paid. Bloom notes, as an aside, that even in the 1960s many probate judges were not lawyers and ran funeral homes on the side; a customer could bargain for a probate-funeral package.

Probate fees are important to many lawyers. They are careful to keep family or other attorneys at bay until the fee is collected. Bloom quotes famed attorney Joseph H. Choate:

> It was one of the brightest members of the profession . . . who had taken his passage for Europe . . . and failed to go. He said one of his rich clients died and he was afraid if he had gone across the Atlantic, the heirs would have gotten all the property.

In June 1975 the Supreme Court ruled that bar associations could no longer set minimum fees. Now shopping for a lawyer is not only possible but prevalent.

A number of other things have also increased competition among lawyers and affected their ability to charge high fees. Some people claim these developments will reduce lawyers' profits, but I doubt it.

First, banks and accountants have entered the estate planning and tax fields, which were once zealously guarded by lawyers as an exclusive province. But then, banks and accountants hire lawyers, anyway.

Second, advertising and publicity, once prohibited, now are legal, as outlined in Chapter 2. Many firms have public relations consultants; many advertise, just like insurance brokers and merchants. But advertising, while it forces fees down, also generates additional business—more wills, more lawsuits, and more work for lawyers.

Third, packaged legal services are beginning to spread. "Five-and-ten" firms such as Jacoby & Meyers (with maybe 300 lawyers and 150 offices) and Hyatt Legal Services (with maybe 700 lawyers and 200 offices) offer wills, divorces, deeds, and the like at standard, fixed fees, affordable by most. Prepaid legal plans, available to perhaps 2 million labor union members, afford similar benefits; maybe as many as 25 million people will have such coverage by 1990. Also, there are union-sponsored "volume discount" plans. Insurance company plans with modest fee schedules are growing. Legal aid clinics are sprouting up. And don't forget H&R Block for personal taxes. But much of this is business that independent lawyers don't want anyway.

More corporations are building larger in-house legal staffs. That is a major trend. Not only do these staffs do legal work that you could do, but they also monitor your fees and try to keep them at a minimum.

An old saw says that if there is only one lawyer in town, he will starve; if there are two, they will prosper. Corporate legal staffs may have this effect. They see more problems and raise more questions. Perhaps as they perform routine legal tasks formerly done by others, they will generate more work for specialists outside, work that might never have been requested without the corporate legal staff to sniff it out.

Other things are contributing in small ways to reduce independent lawyers' fees. No-fault insurance, no-fault divorce, and similar laws are examples. But their effect is small.

Do all these changes prevent you from charging fees that afford you a decent living or even make you wealthy? To the contrary; you still can control your fee income to a large extent.

Once you become famous, you can name your own figure. Louis Nizer, of *My Life in Court* fame, charges maybe $350 an hour. Marty Lipton, a famous takeover specialist, charges $350 an hour, but he tells the client in advance that he may triple this or multiply it by even more if he thinks the result justifies it. Melvin Belli, he of the purple boots and cowboy hat, charges $300 to $350 an hour. Former U.S. Senator Joseph D. Tydings charges $230 an hour. Former Commissioner of Internal Revenue Mortimer Caplin charges more than $300 an hour.

Let's put this in perspective.

Perhaps these hourly fees aren't so large. After all, a fashion model gets from $250 to $400 an hour just for walking down a runway and letting people admire her. Big men with quick reflexes—professional athletes with perhaps a fraction of the brainpower of a good lawyer—may make a million dollars a year. So may women athletes. But on the other hand your secretary makes perhaps ten to twenty-five dollars an hour, depending on her experience and where you practice. An in-house homemaker's aide or nurse earns about seven dollars an hour.

If you charge clients by the hour, be sure to keep good records. The client may ask to see them months later, and although you can refuse, you will probably end up showing them and explaining. So don't write three hours in your diary for "Considering the matter." This will sound to the client months later as if you had your feet on the desk and were gazing at the ceiling or snoozing at his expense. Better say, "Examining cases, dictating letter, writing contract," or something like that.

And be careful how you add up your time. An associate at Cravath, Swaine & Moore charged IBM twenty-seven hours for one day. When queried, he explained that he had worked on a plane going west to California and that the change in time zones enabled him to work for more hours than the clock contains for one day.

Don Santarelli, who founded his own firm in Washington, sent me a news story about a client who received a computer printout along with a $25,532.50 bill. The computer printout showed that the partner involved charged $275 an hour and listed his time as 43.1 hours. The client figured that a one-minute telephone call would have to be "rounded" to six minutes, or one-tenth of an hour, in order to conform to the computer program, and that every minute of "rounding" cost the client $4.58. Moreover, the client was unable to comprehend the fifty cents at the end of the bill, except that the partner's rate of $275 an hour would be equal to fifty cents for every 6.5 seconds, leading the client to believe that there was a second, and secret, computer keeping track of lawyers' time by half-seconds.

Such billings gave rise to the popular story about a lawyer standing at the Pearly Gates who complained that he was too young to have died.

St. Peter replied, "Our records show that you are ninety years old."

"But I'm only forty-eight," the lawyer protested.

"Nope," said St. Peter. "You're ninety years old. We checked the hours you billed to your clients."

One New York law firm became so identified in businessmen's minds as paramount in certain acquisition matters that it began in 1980 to hand potential clients, when they entered the door, a memorandum reading as follows.

Billing Policies

1. Charges for services are based on four factors:
   (i) Time charges (average about $150 per hour)
   (ii) Complexity of matter

(iii) Intensity of the firm's effort

(iv) Result achieved

2. Final charges are a percentage of base time charges and, depending on the other factors, normally range from 100% to 300%. In acquisition transactions where the firm has the responsibility for developing the strategy, final charges are based more heavily on the responsibility assumed and the result achieved and therefore sometimes exceed the upper range.

3. Statements are rendered for each separate matter. The firm does not furnish long-form descriptions of services or details as to particular lawyers and hours.

4. Statements are rendered monthly or at the conclusion of a matter.

5. Monthly statements do not necessarily represent final charges; they are on account of the final charges.

6. The firm does not establish retainer relationships. In certain acquisition matters there is a minimum fee of $50,000–$100,000.

This memorandum was written in 1980. I could not obtain the one in use by the firm today; it must be terrifying! But this memo did not scare clients away. Some decided they needed the firm at any cost.

Rates like this caused Frank Cary, president of IBM during its famous antitrust litigation of the 1970s, to say, "All of our departments have expenditure budgets— except that the legal department has an unlimited budget, and they have already exceeded that."

If your client won't or can't pay these rates, you can try other methods. Some clients prefer an annual retainer. You perform all their services for a flat fee, with specified exceptions such as courtroom litigation. You can charge by the hour, but set a cap on your fee. You can charge different sets of hourly rates, maybe fifty dollars for individuals, a hundred dollars for most corporations, and $150 for rich corporations.

And then there are *contingent fees*. What lawyer hasn't dreamed of suing to recover Manhattan Island for the Indians and getting a one-third contingent fee?

Contigent fees have had an extraordinary impact on our national economy. They have been called "the poor man's key to the courthouse." Because of them, you can sue your dentist, your grocer, your doctor, an entire airline, the plane manufacturer, your accountant, and so on. Even a friend who invites you over for a cocktail. In New York City many small landlords refuse to rent apartments to young lawyers for fear of a lawsuit at the first inconvenience.

And—horror of horrors—anyone now can sue lawyers, tit for tat. They can and sometimes will sue you. Alas, malpractice insurance for lawyers in New York costs $2,500 per lawyer for $5 million of coverage, with $250,000 deductible. You may be sued for a lot more than $5 million.

In Antioch, California, a car of beer-drinking teenagers struck a light pole. Lawyers on a contingent fee basis sued everyone—the driver, the city of Antioch itself, a nearby shopping center, even the utility company that owned the light pole. In Pittsburgh a man died of leukemia; the lawyer for his widow claimed that his death was caused by exposure to benzine. He brought a suit against all 101 companies that manufacture benzine, although most of these patently had no connection with the matter. Over 10 percent of all dentists have claims pending against them; large awards are always possible because of jurors' natural fear of dentists. Some of this inundation of contingent fee suits is lessened by state laws against frivolous suits and, since 1983, by federal judges occasionally making the lawyers themselves pay a defendant's legal fees if the suit is declared frivolous.

At the University of Wisconsin a study showed that most contingent fee suits involve small claims—less than $10,000. Only 12 percent involve claims of over $50,000.

But *mass torts* can involve huge amounts. And even

small firms or sole practitioners can bring suits for victims of mass torts, such as an airplane crash, asbestos poisoning, toxic shock syndrome, and maybe even cigarettes or cobalt. Someone estimated that contingent fees of 40 percent or more might result in a number of small law firms collecting fees of $80 million each or thereabouts for asbestos settlements in cases now pending alone. Imagine yourself with an $80 million fee, all in cash. Contingent fees in the Johns Manville asbestos cases totaled about $1 billion, and Manville was only part of the industry.

A sole practitioner can sue Manville for one injured client or twenty, just like a larger firm.

Union Carbide's plant in Bhopal, India, leaked a poisonous gas that killed 2,000 people and injured thousands more. Claims exceed $3 billion; lawyers both from the United States and from India purport to represent claimants. A one-third contingent fee?

Contingent-fee suits may be having an almost equal impact in the area of corporate responsibility. *Strike suits* can be brought against major corporations in the name of a shareholder with only one or two shares. And small law firms probably bring more such suits than large law firms. Major accounting firms are sued. Arthur Anderson, an accounting firm, paid $137 million in out-of-court settlements between 1980 and 1985. Even that didn't entitle Arthur Anderson to a breather. And in 1986 it was sued for more than $800 million in connection with its audit of John DeLorean's famous gull-winged sports-car venture. Major investment bankers, major law firms—none are immune.

Such havoc—as it seems to defendants—has been caused that insurance is no longer a protection. Insurance companies themselves have been wrecked. Lloyds of London syndicates have been shaken, one of them broken. Insurance for asbestos liability is not available. Insurance premiums for accountants, lawyers, and directors have doubled and tripled and quadrupled. Some directors' insurance has increased tenfold. My own law firm dropped its directors' insurance, and the partners resigned all directorships unless the corporations which they served carried insurance for them.

Johns Manville, once a tower of financial strength, went into bankruptcy because of asbestos-related lawsuits. G. D. Searle halted sales in the United States of its IUD contraceptive—which had been used by 1 million American women, approved by the FDA, and endorsed by Planned Parenthood—because of "unwarranted lawsuits" and the mushrooming cost "just to keep a file warm in some lawyer's office." The Searle IUD continues to be used in one hundred other countries, including by 60 million Chinese women, but it is no longer available to American women.

Skating rinks close because they can't afford new premiums. "White-water" boating resorts close. Doctors retire to safety at home. A fire-alarm company cannot get insurance at any price. A doctor in New York with no insurance committed suicide apparently because of a suit brought on a contingency-fee basis. And believe it or not, last year nearly $100 million in judgments were rendered against clergymen and their flocks!

The disorder caused by proliferating lawsuits may be why lawyers need three patron saints instead of just one. They are Saint Ivo Helory, Saint Thomas More (for Catholic lawyers), and Saint Nicholas of Myra. (The latter is, by coincidence or higher plan, also the patron saint of thieves and pawnbrokers.)

Contingent fees made possible the litigation that caused all this. But used wisely by you, they can also be your financial making.

A few more words about fees: Try always to have a written agreement about them; clients forget quickly. Collect them in advance where possible, or as quickly as possible otherwise; they become harder to collect later.

And beware of taking stock, partnership interests, and

the like. Probably 75 percent of all new businesses fail to make the grade, and you will end up doing a lot of work for nothing.

My Uncle John once told me about his collection problems. I told him I had heard of lawyers taking stock for fees and that the client turned out to be IBM or Exxon. The lawyers turned into multimillionaires.

Uncle John laughed at this story. He said, "Harry, Jr., that happens once in a million times. I've taken stock in hundreds of companies, I guess, and none of them amounted to much.

"In fact, I've got a whole drawer full of worthless stock certificates I took for legal fees. Here, look at all these worthless certificates."

And he pulled open a drawer and waved at it with a pained expression, hurt at the thought of the worthless stock. He glanced into the drawer. His pained expression slowly changed to a smile, then a grin.

"Wrong drawer," he said. "Those fees were paid in full."

I looked into the drawer. There were no stock certificates—just bottles of white lightning.

◆◆◆◆◆◆◆

There once was a time, within memory of some lawyers still practicing, when attorneys would happily accept eggs, chickens, or moonshine liquor as payment for their services.

Those days are gone. Today fees paid in dollars are high and getting higher.

How much should you, as a lawyer just starting your own firm, charge for your services? As is usually the case, there is no easy answer, but some comparisons may provide a few guidelines.

The hourly charge for a high-ranking partner's services in New York City today may be well over $260; a senior partner may take home more than $1 million a year. On the other hand, a firm offering packaged legal services may charge a flat fee of fifty dollars or so for drawing up a will, and its attorneys are rewarded commensurately.

One law firm charged according to four factors: the time spent on the case, the complexity of the matter, the intensity of the firm's efforts, and the result achieved. That's one method you might consider. And then, of course, there are annual retainers, contingent fees, and other methods of payment.

Regardless of what you charge, here are some good rules: Put the agreement in writing. Collect fees in advance, if possible, or as quickly as possible if that's not feasible. Forget about accepting stock, partnership interests, or other forms of barter in payment for your services. Stick to cash.

6

PEOPLE, EQUIP-MENT, AND OTHER ESSENTIALS

One night in June 1980 I was sitting at home reading a book when the phone rang. It was my good friend and client Dr. Leo Winter, who heads the medical research company bearing his name. Leo's distaste for lawyers was almost an obsession, but for once he sounded cheery. He even chuckled as he spoke.

"Turn on the news, quick!" Leo said.

"Why?" I asked, reaching for the TV switch.

"Your office is on fire!" He laughed.

The TV screen lighted up. There was my office building, 299 Park Avenue in New York City, with flames leaping out of the 20th- and 21st-floor windows. It was just like the movie *Towering Inferno*. It was spectacular—and numbing.

The next morning we gathered on the sidewalk across the street, blocked from the building by firemen's lines. It was obvious by ten o'clock that we were not going to use the premises again for weeks or months. We had no office. What to do?

By noon we had rented bedrooms and dining rooms—

anything we could—in the nearby Barclay Hotel, and everyone was busy. Rented typewriters appeared. Telephone numbers of clients were divided up. Lawyers dictated while lying on beds, apparently enjoying it. Secretaries sat on the floors in blue jeans, dictation pads in their laps. Messengers opened doors, said, "Excuse me," and rushed to the next room. Some of the younger lawyers dashed off to the bar association library. An insurance examiner poked around. Harried clients rushed in and out.

Dr. Winter appeared, opening doors, still laughing. "Burned the rascals out," he said, and laughed some more.

A couple of months later, I compared the hourly time charges for the two weeks after the fire with those for two weeks before. They were only slightly smaller.

In other words we had practiced law in completely makeshift quarters, without word processors, photocopiers, computers, data transmission equipment, our own library, or most of our files. And we had been able to work almost as many hours, almost as efficiently, under these adverse conditions.

What does that prove? It shows that you can start your law firm with as little office space and equipment as you want. You don't have to make a big deal out of it.

When the British company Hanson Trust acquired control of U.S. Industries in 1984 in a hostile takeover, Hanson proceeded to discharge or "lose" more than 120 of the 125 U.S. Industries employees at its Stamford headquarters. Two of the senior lawyers who shared this fate, Doug Craig and Ted Ells, decided after considerable thought to form the law firm of Craig & Ells.

Once that decision was made, they set about to undertake the chores physically necessary to open an office, anticipating that it would require about a week or so. As it turned out, searching for office space alone took over a month, and it was some time before they realized that different real estate agents were showing them office space they had already seen.

That was just the beginning. After the office space was acquired, they had to worry about painting, acquiring furniture, and purchasing photocopying equipment and word processors—an infinite number of details. The installation of telephones became so snarled that they had to retain an expert to deal with the telephone company to get both of the phones in place.

When they had completed most of these tangible matters, they turned their attention to other essentials such as being listed in directories, obtaining service contracts for the duplicating machines, payroll taxes, medical taxes, occupancy taxes, and the like. They acquired insurance of various kinds. The most important was malpractice insurance, which is very expensive, but they also got fire, business interruption, general liability (failing clients and the like), loss of valuable papers, and umbrella policies. Employee bonds and workers' compensation insurance would come later.

It took them six weeks to get a painter to put their name on the door.

After all this was finished, they discovered twelve picture hooks protruding from their walls. So together they selected twelve pictures—one for each hook. Today, when someone asks, "Why do you have a picture in that odd place in the corner?" Craig answers matter-of-factly, "Because there was a hook there."

During this process, they discovered still more things they needed. They hadn't thought of a toilet, a stepladder, pencil sharpeners, announcements to be mailed, and other mundane but necessary matters.

Then clients began slowly to come in. There was a Turkish art dealer who wanted to syndicate each oil painting as he purchased it abroad for resale here, promising the investors a 20 percent profit in sixty days; he asked Craig & Ells to help him get the investors together. There was an operator of a chain of gay bathhouses.

Then one day a man walked in (they had no receptionist at the beginning) and told Ted Ells that he had come to sell him a menorah, a Jewish candelabrum, which he displayed proudly.

Ells said, "I am not Jewish."

The man replied, "But aren't you the Weinstein whose name I saw on the directory downstairs?"

They had forgotten to change the names in the lobby directory.

Craig said he sometimes envies a well-known divorce lawyer who has his only office in Garden City, Long Island, but comes to New York City once a day and meets women clients in the lobby of the Yale Club.

"No fuss, no bother," explains Craig. "The Yale Club makes a great office."

Leonard Sims, who had also been in the U.S. Industries legal department before the hostile takeover, conducted his affairs on a simpler level. He practiced law from his Manhattan apartment. No worry about office space, office furniture, office equipment, office telephones; he just used what was already there.

Secretaries are called in on a temporary basis when needed; a telephone answering machine takes messages; photocopying is done at the corner drug store. Sims licks stamps.

Except for living expenses, no capital is needed, and there is no fixed overhead. His only visits to the outside world occur when he has to appear in court or use the bar association library.

For lunch he often cooks on a grill on his own terrace. For exercise he goes to the swimming pool in the basement of his apartment building, where until recently he occasionally swam with Hedy Lamarr, the screen siren.

Sims's girlfriend is a doctor, so presumably he doesn't go out for medical treatment. He says, "I've got it all right here. And my clients don't give a hoot about a fancy Park Avenue office. They want *me*, not the office."

Would a house in the country suit your needs?

Larry Machiz worked for a large firm in New York, but his wife was from a small town; she and their two small sons were not happy with apartment life. So Larry bought a farmhouse in Malden Bridge, New York, 150 miles from New York City, population fifty families. He installed a computer for word processing and telecommunicating with law firms in New York City.

The Manhattan firms treat him as a "contract associate" and send him real estate business of various kinds by computer or overnight mail; he bills the firms on an hourly basis. Of his new life he says, "New York firms give me business because I am too far away to steal their clients. They would avoid me like the plague if I lived nearby."

As for office staffing, Larry says, "I like typing my own letters because there is no secretary to go home and abandon me and there is no head of the word processing department to fuss with me for redoing a letter too many times. I am totally in control of my own documents."

He thought for a moment and then added, "Of course, I didn't foresee that my two little boys would run through my office whenever their games made it necessary, and I haven't quite mastered that distraction yet."

Would a part-time office suit your needs?

Tony Ambrosio was assistant corporation counsel in Newark at a salary of $15,000 a year. He decided he wanted his own law practice. He made a deal with a sole practitioner to use the latter's telephone and office at lunchtime and nights and weekends for sixty dollars a month. Then he started his own part-time practice with clients such as a paraplegic who had been shot by a girlfriend's father who lived in her cellar, a voodooist who paid legal fees with newly printed hundred-dollar bills, and numerous drunken drivers and criminals. In five years the annual fees from his private practice grew from $10,000 to $50,000. He quit the assistant corporation counsel job and helped form the Newark firm Ambrosio, Kyreakakis & DiLorenzo, with luxurious quarters and income to match. He has come a long way from his original sixty-dollar-a-month part-time rental deal.

Perhaps the limit on how far you can go was demonstrated by a wire-cutting firm in Chicago, which for an annual rent of 75 cents a square foot set up its office in an abandoned men's toilet. The office contains a desk, a chair, toilet piping behind the desk, and an unflushable urinal on the wall. The office space nearby costs twenty dollars a square foot.

Don't overdo equipment buying. When my own office first opened, my partner Paul Chase bought a powerful paper shredder worthy of the CIA and placed it smack on top of his desk. "It's to destroy 'secret papers,' " he explained. For the next twenty years I never saw or heard of any "secret papers" calling for a shredder of that power, and I think it never was used except to shred newspapers as a demonstration for curious clients. Or perhaps Paul received many secret love letters, but if so, he had a lot more admirers than I ever found out about.

Once you get the questions of office space and equipment behind you, your next necessity will probably be a secretary. If you are a lone practitioner, you should seek someone who is a combination secretary, telephone operator, file clerk, paralegal, and, in a pinch, a stand-in lawyer.

I suppose all male lawyers beginning a practice have fantasized about having a secretary straight out of a James Bond movie, such as Pussy Galore might have been—and female lawyers, having Agent 007 himself as a secretary.

It doesn't work that way.

In the first place, remember that Jimmy Carter said regretfully, "I have lusted in my heart." First of all, lust, even when just in your heart, doesn't mix with a start-up law practice. A moonstruck lawyer is apt to make goofs if his or her mind is where it shouldn't be. And a new practice is no place for goofs. Maybe you can afford a few later on, when you are established, but not in the beginning. Like President Carter, you'd regret it.

Second, if your secretary looks like Pussy Galore or James Bond, there is certain to be competition and even jealousy. This is bad enough if the jealous one is your own partner, but it is worse if it is your best client. You may wind up losing your secretary or your client or both.

Third, other kinds of disasters may occur.

Here is an extreme example. It occurred at Christmastime in 1982. A female clerk word processor allegedly shot and killed a male partner at the staid Fifth Avenue law firm Burke & Burke after stalking him through three rooms of the office. *The New York Times* reported that the clerk cited a romantic affair as the reason for the shooting; maybe in her mind such an affair had occurred. Others said the size of her Christmas bonus may have been the cause.

It could happen to you.

So perhaps you should have a secretary-helper-assistant of your own sex. I had a male secretary, Jim Keane, for twenty-two years, and that probably saved me a lot of grief. Nor did I ever experience any grief with my three subsequent female secretaries, but of course I was older then and possibly less foolish.

I must say, as an aside, that my present secretary, Janet, is the best of them all. But then, she has a husband who has priorities and rights; Jim Keane had no wife. Janet seems to me to be on vacation about six months a year, although our office manager has confirmed to me that it is only four weeks—or maybe the two of them are in cahoots. But who's to complain? A poor secretary of either sex wouldn't be missed by a lawyer, but the absence of a top-notch secretary can mean havoc.

If you don't feel a defensive need to have a same-sex

secretary, then by all means seek an attractive person of the other sex—but only if that person has all the *real* qualifications for the job. It's a big job: dictation, typing, handling clients, setting up and maintaining file systems. It requires stamina, patience, diligence, and diplomacy. In a start-up office, this person is a huge part of your life, so take plenty of time and care in finding him or her. Paying a few extra dollars a week, if necessary, may be the best investment you ever make.

Later on, if your firm grows, there'll be many other non-lawyer personnel—switchboard operators, accountants, paralegals, word processors, mailroom personnel, messengers, duplicating-room personnel, personnel managers, department chiefs, and so on. Of course, at first you can get some of these on a part-time basis—temporary secretaries or temporary accountants and the like.

Eventually, however, you'll find yourself needing a professional office manager. In smaller firms one of the secretaries may rise to this position. As the firm continues to grow, the Peter Principle (promotion to the point where one doesn't have the ability to perform) may come into play and the ex-secretary may prove inadequate. Of course, some professionally trained office managers earn $50,000 a year; a few in the megafirms make several times that.

Sometimes a sort of reverse of the Peter Principle can occur. You may find that you are constitutionally unable to delegate authority to an office manager after once having done everything yourself. You may stick your nose into the smallest details even though you are paying somebody else a handsome salary to handle them and they can handle them better than you, and even though you could make more money spending that time on a client's matter. I have seen some of my own partners spend literally hours on trivial administrative problems; they stuck their noses into the problems even though they were somebody else's business and were being properly handled. They—and all of us—would be better off without this, but unfortunately some or most lawyers never outgrow their roles as sole or beginning entrepreneurs. They remain like kids counting marbles when they should be doing real chores.

Janet Lewis, office manager at Barnett & Alagia in Washington, once said, "Too often lawyers simply can't delegate. They have got to learn how to turn over the small mundane details. . . . You find, as an administrator, that you nod your head a lot, and then go ahead and do it your way." So tell your professional office manager, if you get one, what his or her role is, and then let him or her do it. You practice law.

Whether you have a staff of one, a girl or boy Friday, or a large number of people, remember that they are human beings just like you. It is not uncommon to hear a lawyer give instructions to his secretary in an imperious manner, to issue orders to an accountant as if the latter were a personal servant, or to curse a messenger.

Don't do it. Lawyers who behave in such a fashion are known behind their backs as "crazies." Unfortunately, there are plenty of them around. And they cause a loss of morale, sometimes even the loss of valuable personnel. I have known paralegals to leave because a lawyer sent them on too many personal errands. Maybe who gets the coffee isn't really a matter of life or death, but sending a paralegal out with your dirty laundry is a serious offense. You may lose that paralegal soon.

A more remote, but also potentially disasterous, possibility is that the employee you offend today may become important to you tomorrow. Suppose an offended employee gets a job with a client and you have to plead with him or her for an appointment. Or suppose he or she goes to work for a competitor, where another kind of dirty laundry may be involved. That defector may someday have your fate securely in his or her hands. Gilbert and Sullivan put it this way:

> *When I was a lad I served a term*
> *As office boy to an Attorney's firm.*
> *I cleaned the windows and I swept the floor*
> *And I polished up the handle of the big front door*
> *I polished up that handle so carefullee*
> *That now I am the Ruler of the Queen's Navee!*

Probably your office worker will not become Secretary of the Navy. But might he or she not become, say, a judge before whom you try a case?

Consider that Abe Hummel started at age thirteen as an office boy to William Howe. By 1869, in six years, he rose to be an infamous partner in the infamous firm of Howe & Hummel.

Pam Pierson, a lawyer at San Francisco's Schapiro and Thorn, began as a secretary at the mighty firm Pillsbury, Madison & Sutro.

Fanny Holtzman, the famous entertainment lawyer, was a clerk-secretary for a law firm. On her graduation from Fordham Law School in 1922, she opened her own office. She immediately hired her former boss, a partner from that law firm, to work for her as an associate lawyer!

Many secretaries have gone on to achieve success beyond the office world. Samuel Insull, creator of a huge utility pyramid that collapsed in the Great Depression, started out as secretary to Thomas Alva Edison. Charles Dickens was a court secretary before be became Britain's premier novelist. Billy Rose was a secretary before he became the best-known producer on Broadway after Flo Ziegfeld. Better that these people remember you favorably.

If you had a secretary who looked like Pussy Galore and then went on to Hollywood, would you want her to tell a gossip columnist that you stank as a boss? Or would you prefer the fellows in the country club locker room to read how much Pussy enjoyed working for you?

If things go well for you, you'll hire other lawyers. Not only can that be critical to the present success of the firm, it can make a difference in whether the firm lives on after you retire.

You have many choices here. How about an experienced lawyer who can do the same kinds of things you do and who can fill in for you? Or how about a lawyer experienced in a different field who could add diversity to your practice? Or an attorney with a number of clients to enlarge your own practice? Or a brilliant young lawyer with no experience but with the promise of becoming a world-beater? Or a workhorse type, not brilliant, but who can learn to free you from the drudgery that takes up too much of your time, leaving you to attend to more important matters?

Maybe Justice Oliver Wendell Holmes would be a misfit in your firm. Only you can figure out what you need to get where you want to go.

Go slow in deciding; take your time. It's difficult to unravel things if you make a mistake in hiring or joining another lawyer. Remember the lawsuits between Melvin Belli and the lawyers who once were in his office. Remember that similar suits have afflicted even large Wall Street-type firms such as Finley, Kumble. Remember the break-up of some firms and the resulting bitterness and financial losses. It's better to skip over one or two good people than to make a mistake, at least during your start-up.

Once you have grown enough to hire other lawyers, you will be in the *leverage* business. Leverage is an old concept among larger law firms across the country. Simply put, it means that you charge more for associate lawyers than their salaries and overhead cost you, thus leaving a profit for yourself. The same is true, of course, of paralegals and junior partners.

Say that you have three associates each at $40,000 a year, and assume overhead of $20,000 each. You charge

$80,000 a year for them, or about fifty dollars an hour, assuming they work 1,600 billable hours a year (a little under 35 hours a week). That leaves you a profit of $20,000 on each of your associates, or $60,000 before you have charged anything for your own time. Let's say you now charge a hundred dollars an hour for *your* time. That's $160,000 a year. Assume overhead of $40,000, and you're left with a total profit of $180,000—more than your own gross billings!

If you are going into leveraging, you have to pay the young lawyers. How much? Why not try zero? If you are looking for relatively unskilled assistance, a zero starting salary may be possible. Many recent law school graduates are unemployed, and some of them would love to gain experience and perhaps earn a little on their own cases, if any, in hopes of getting a salary later on—or, in time, of starting their own practices. This is not as rare as you might suppose, even in the high-salary area of New York City.

If you have to pay a salary to an associate lawyer or lawyers, you will find a wide range in every city. In Manhattan some one-person firms probably pay less than one-tenth the salaries being paid in the same city by the giant corporate law firms. Of course, the latter will hire the top of the class from the best law schools, but maybe you don't need that just yet. And a lot of the salary you pay can be contingent on earnings or contingent on one case or otherwise variable.

There are two major methods of training young lawyers.

The Cravath method, famous since the turn of the century, is to closely supervise the work of a young lawyer on a clearly defined question, one small area of the whole case. When he or she has mastered that, assign the lawyer to other tasks; eventually the whole will be learned.

The Buckner method, named for former New York District Attorney Emory Buckner, is almost the reverse.

The young attorney is given immediate responsibility for a whole case or for a large part of it; he or she is left alone. The lawyer's progress to larger cases depends on how he or she does alone on smaller ones.

The difference was best illustrated when my partner, Jack O'Donnell, was talking with Cravath partner Ralph McAfee. Word processing machines had just come into vogue, and O'Donnell became excited upon learning what they could do. He was working on a matter with McAfee and couldn't resist bragging about the new machine.

"Hey, Ralph!" said O'Donnell. "We have a new machine that will do everything you tell it to. If you want to capitalize a particular word all the way through a one-hundred-page brief, you just push some buttons, and the machine capitalizes that word everywhere it appears. How about that?"

McAfee replied with appropriate Cravath disdain, "Why, Jack, we have lots of those around here. We call them associates."

I'm sure McAfee was twitting O'Donnell; Cravath treats its young associates in every way as full-fledged lawyers with the respect due a member of the Bar. McAfee indicated clearly that attention to detail is a Cravath trademark from day one.

Should you adopt the Cravath method or the Buckner method? That depends on the aptitude of your young lawyer or lawyers. It also depends on your own teaching ability. Which method do you prefer? Which suits your own style?

It also depends on clients' preferences, since they may object to whatever status you give associates in their affairs. You'll have to take each case on its own for a while, until your firm sets a policy.

And don't forget that a good paralegal is as good as, or better than, a young lawyer for much legal work—and much cheaper.

Paralegals are particularly suitable when the firm's

business is highly specialized. My daughter Bonnie and three others formed a new firm in Raleigh called Yates, Fleishman, McLamb & Weyher to represent defendants in product liability, medical malpractice, and related matters. She herself specializes in defending insurance companies in arson cases. These almost always involve jury trials; the pattern of the cases is much alike. Paralegals can do much of the work usually done by lawyers, such as preparing interrogatories, indexing evidence, and the like. The client insurance companies love this arrangement because they see the cheaper hourly rates of the paralegals on their computer printout bills.

I talked to one of Bonnie's female paralegals one day to see how much she had learned about her specialty and to find out whether I could compare the paralegal to a lawyer doing the same work.

"Oh, these cases are all very much alike," the paralegal said.

"In what way?"

"Well, for example, when a new arson case comes in involving a house, you can tell immediately whether the fire was set by the husband or the wife."

"You can?" I asked. "How?"

"It's easy. The husband might torch a house anywhere— the attic, the cellar, or anywhere. But the wife always torches it in only two places."

"Where?" I asked.

"In their bedroom or in the husband's clothes closet."

Such attention to patterns of behavior and details can make a big difference in the way a paralegal prepares interrogatories and in which facts he or she takes care to index. In this context a good, observant paralegal can be invaluable. This one was a good one—the equal of a lawyer for this work.

After assembling all this apparatus—getting together the office and equipment and people—should you incorporate? Or should you practice as a sole proprietor, or partnership?

None of the megafirms of the big cities have incorporated, although some of their individual partners may incorporate. But a good many smaller firms *have* incorporated. Why?

One reason for incorporation, which occurs to the clients and may give them pause, is that the lawyer gets limited liability. In most states a lawyer's personal assets, outside the corporation, cannot be reached by creditors except in the case of the lawyer's own malpractice or the malpractice of lawyers he supervised. The lawyer may escape personal liability for the malpractice of his partners.

In these days of intense competition and advertising and openly soliciting business, it would not be surprising to hear a lawyer tell a client the half truth that a competing lawyer has incorporated because "he's afraid of malpractice liability—you know, wants to protect his assets."

A second and more important reason for incorporation has been the fringe benefits available to incorporated lawyers. These once included tax deductions for larger pension plans, life insurance premiums, reimbursable medical expense plans, and disability insurance. In some cases state taxes could be reduced and more favorable tax years could be elected. The bulk, but not all, of these tax advantages have lessened or vanished over the years. For the newly started practitioner, incorporation is not the panacea it once seemed. Run over the figures with your accountant (or your new secretary, if he or she knows a little bookkeeping), and see what dollars might be saved in your own case.

As your new practice grows, you'll want to review administrative matters regularly.

One friend of mine, on graduation from law school,

opened an office. After two years he had taken on two partners, four associates, five secretary-stenographers, and a couple of other employees. Excluding partners, there were now eleven employees.

He decided, like New York's Mayor Edward I. Koch, to ask "How'm I doing?" So he compiled a questionnaire to be returned unsigned, asking about his management, and he circulated the questionnaire to the eleven employees.

He received twelve replies from the eleven employees. Eleven replies were complimentary. The twelfth, written in untraceable block letters, said, "You creeps don't know your ass from a hole in the ground."

Because that questionnaire produced an unexpected reply, it turned up a disgruntled employee. In such a case either you are doing something wrong or there is a rotten apple that could spoil the barrel. So by all means continually check with the employees as to their perspective on your law practice—and move quickly to heed their suggestions and views.

Not long ago I was at home one night when the phone rang. It was my good friend and client Dr. Leo Winter, who has such a distaste for lawyers.

"Say, I want you to come over for dinner Thursday."

"Sure, I'd like to. Is it anything special?" I asked.

"Yeah, it sure is. Don't you know Thursday is Halloween?" He laughed loudly.

"What about Halloween?"

"Well, the goblins and witches are out, and the evil spirits. But I'm too old now to dress up and go out and scare people. So I'm going to do it right here at home." He laughed uproariously.

"Who are you going to scare?" I asked.

"You," he said. "I videotaped your office building burning a few years ago, and I remember how worried you were when you rented those temporary rooms at the Barclay. So I'm going to show you the movies of that fire and scare the hell out of you again. I loved every minute of it."

Then he paused and added quietly, "But you fellows did get along pretty well without an office."

◆◆◆◆◆◆◆

Right from the beginning, you'll need people—or at least one person—furnishings, and equipment for your new business. Your first necessity may be a secretary, and if you're smart, you'll look for one who can be simultaneously a typist, telephone operator, organizer, file clerk, paralegal, and even a stand-in lawyer—not necessarily in that order. Later you may need accountants, word processors, personnel managers, an office manager, and others. Keep your hiring to a minimum, but if you do need assistance, be sure to give these people the respect and authority they need to get their jobs done properly.

Choosing the proper furniture and quarters may seem terribly important at first, but never forget that they are only tools to be operated by living, breathing, thinking human beings. Successful law practices can be conducted from telephone booths, crowded offices—even an abandoned men's room. So get your priorities straight, and never forget that an ounce of brains at work is worth a ton of furniture and equipment.

7

GENERAL PRACTICE

Shortly after I finished law school, I dropped in on a friend of mine, Bud Williams, who had also just graduated. Bud had opened his own office in a small North Carolina town, and I wanted to see what beginning a practice was like.

When I walked into Bud's office, I saw that it consisted of one room, with a desk for Bud, a large work table, and the beginnings of a library. There was no secretary, no reception room—that was it. On the work table I saw a number of crude drawings, but I couldn't make out what they were.

"What are you doing?" I asked after some opening banter.

"Well, my cousin is an architect, and he's trying to get his client to let me do the legal work—buying the land, working out a construction contract, that sort of thing. t'll be my first client."

"That's great," I said. "When will you know about it?"

"Well, that depends on whether the client likes my

cousin's plans for the house. If she likes the plans, we'll get rolling. And I can't wait."

"Terrific! That first client seems to take forever, but eventually the first one comes."

"Yeah, I've heard that. Come over here and look at these. I didn't have anything else to do, so I sketched up my ideas about the house, and I'm going to give them to my cousin the architect. I think the ideas will help him a lot. He doesn't really understand the problems."

"What problems?" I asked.

"Well you see, this house would be for Rebecca Trice. You know her, don't you?"

Rebecca Trice! I sure knew who she was. Her reputation was exceptional. She ran, by consensus, the finest red-light house east of Greensboro. She was famous for her contributions to local charities and for helping her girls along at the local bank with loans and things like that. I had seen her in the bank.

"Is that what these sketches are about?" I asked. "They look like the Pentagon, but there are more sides."

"Yes, you've got to have lots of rooms in a good red-light house. Separate living rooms for different groups, plenty of bathrooms, and the like. You don't need many closets. Just clothes trees. I've been working on these plans for two weeks, and I think I've got it all figured out. Even separate garages, so nobody can copy your auto license number. And a separate entrance for the girls and for services like food, whiskey, laundry, and so forth."

"Lord, I didn't think law practice would be like this," I said.

"Well, when you start on a client, you like to really dig in and try to be valuable to that client, and that's what I'm doing. I'm not just copying an old deed—going through the motions. I'm putting out for this job."

"I can see you are," I said. "And what are all these hatch marks around the sides of the building?"

Bud gave me a wise and knowing look. He said, "Those are exits. In a red-light house, you need lots of exits—lots and lots of exits."

I wouldn't advise helping clients with plans that skirt the law, but if you start a general practice, you have to be ready for anything. Your previous training and experience may have no bearing on what you will be doing in your own law practice.

How do you decide whether to go into a general practice or to specialize? What specialty should you choose? Or do you have that choice? Do your law school and work background predetermine the nature of your practice? Or does a chain of unknown future events, combined with your aptitudes, determine the nature of your practice?

None of these questions can be answered categorically. Probably your law school training will not be an important factor. One cannot really learn a specialty in law school, except perhaps by way of a second law school degree—a master of laws or doctor of laws with a specialty.

Your work experience after law school may be more significant. Perhaps you have learned a specialty and earned a reputation to go with it. Possibly a few clients will follow you from contacts made while working, whether at a law firm or for the government or at a corporation. These factors probably will dictate your course, at least at the beginning.

If your start-up commences just after law school, or if the factors above do not come into play, probably you will follow the course indicated by the needs of your clients, whoever they are. If you are faced with a multitude of unrelated questions from a variety of clients, you'll tend toward a general practice.

Of course, other circumstances might cause you to specialize immediately.

If your family controls a large corporation, for example, you might immediately begin to specialize in corporate law. If you have friends who can assure you a steady flow of litigation, you might start out specializing in some type of trial work. Rebecca Trice could have supplied a flow of arrest cases to Bud Williams, had he chosen that direction.

Or you might have an uncle who imports bicycles and assigns you all the injury cases arising from defective bicycles. An accountant friend might find you tax cases; you could immediately begin to specialize in taxes.

But barring special circumstances of that sort, you probably will take on all kinds of cases, at least at first, and be a general practitioner. This may sound like a come-down—a less exalted status than the specialist. It is not.

Think of your tax specialist friends, for example. Would they have the versatility, patience, resourcefulness, decisiveness and confidence to handle Bud Williams's real estate matter? Could they represent a defendant in an assault case? Could they sue a husband for a divorce?

Would you let them handle the case if your little sister were arrested on a drug charge? What if a neighbor shot your dog? Would you want them to help you exact revenge on a "friend" who knocked you down during a drunken party at the country club?

Unless the tax lawyers are unusual, you probably wouldn't pick them for many of these cases, if any. But a general practitioner has to deal with them all.

Indeed, he or she has to be ready to face wholly new problems at any time, even after years of practice. There are always new laws, new people, new circumstances, and new moral standards.

This is a constantly changing world. That's nothing new. I've heard that the first person to say "Things change fast" was Adam as he and Eve were leaving the Garden of Eden.

Many general practitioners have found themselves at some point suing on behalf of a hapless husband for alienation of his wife's affections, and at a later point turning around and suing another hapless husband on behalf of an alienator he had assaulted.

It's the same with farmers. *Specialist* tractor-drivers moving from farm to farm do nothing but drive tractors. Sometimes they pull a sod-breaker, a disc, or a pesticide sprayer; sometimes a combine. But always they drive the tractor.

Generalist farmers, however, must do many things. Perhaps their need for a tractor is limited, so it's more economical to rent a tractor or maybe even use a mule—just as generalist lawyers use a smaller library or have less access to equipment or even human assistance. But generalist farmers, unlike specialist tractor-drivers, also must milk the cows (or maybe goats), feed the hogs, collect the eggs, set traps for the foxes, poison the moles, know when to plow in rainy weather, lay irrigation lines, dig ditches, fence land, deal with the bankers, and maybe build an outhouse or a tool shed. They often have to rely on makeshift tools. They often work in the middle of the night or in bad weather.

The specialist does not need as much versatility, patience, resourcefulness, decisiveness, or confidence.

The difference between specialist lawyers and general practitioners can be tested in a direct way if you have the heart for it. This test is almost surefire.

Assume that a tax specialist, a corporate lawyer, and a litigator are at a cocktail party with a general practitioner and that you don't know which is which. When you enter the room, go up to the group with a cocktail in your hand and talk about almost any current subject, such as the underlying causes of starvation in Ethiopia, the prevalence of AIDS, a Broadway play, or one of the downfalls of Billy Martin as manager of the Yankees.

How do you know which is which? Well, the tax specialist will probably stare at the ceiling as if nothing had been said; the corporate lawyer will repeat what you said but recast your language to make the sentences much longer and to use more words; and the litigator will contradict you and then change the subject to something he or she knows better.

By contrast, the general practitioner will enter into a civilized flow of conversation on whatever topic you raise. Not only do they have wider experience, so that they are more likely to know what you are talking about, but they are accustomed to having the unknown suddenly thrown at them and are adept at handling it.

If a woman enjoys going to cocktail parties and requires an escort, she is far more likely to find an agreeable one from among the general practitioners. And the same goes for a man seeking a date with a female lawyer—at least for the first date.

What kinds of things do general practitioners actually do every day? And is the scope of their practices likely to change over the years?

It would be informative to look at the firm Howe & Hummel. That firm was organized in 1869 at 89 Centre Street in New York City by William F. Howe, a large man given to very loud dress and much jewelry, and his younger partner, Abraham Hummel.

They were an odd couple indeed. Hummel, in contrast to Howe, was five feet tall, had a large bald head, and was partial to funereal black suits and a derby.

Theirs was a general practice firm at first. They worked on contracts of various kinds, and they also handled wills, trusts, and estates. Trial work of various sorts also came their way. You might have a general practice just about like it.

As happens to so many general practitioners, Howe & Hummel evolved over the years from this general practice into a specialist firm. Theirs was two-pronged.

The first specialty became any kind of law involving morals, such as criminal law, divorce suits, bastardy cases, and the like. As Howe & Hummel became more and more famous in this field, it became more flamboyant. Eventually the firm had its name on a sign over its door perhaps thirty feet long. The cable address was LENIENT.

When 74 madams were arrested in a public drive in 1884, each and every one of them named Howe & Hummel, which had by then been in business 15 years, as her counsel. Howe & Hummel, during its existence, defended more than a thousand people indicted for murder or manslaughter. They so dominated the field that their only significant competition was Abraham Levy, known as "The Last Hope," who defended a mere 300 persons indicted for murder or manslaughter.

Their second specialty was the entertainment business. Howe & Hummel did legal work for celebrities such as P. T. Barnum, Edwin Booth, John Drew, the young John Barrymore, Little Egypt, Lillie Langtry, Stanford White, John L. Sullivan, and Lillian Russell. Most of it had to do with show business. In 1893 the firm was said to have grossed $250,000, believed to be the largest annual income of any American law firm at that time.

Your own general practice probably will not be as glittering and sordid as that of Howe & Hummel, but it could be every bit as exciting and stimulating.

I've mentioned several kinds of matters that may come your way, but there are many others. What of estates and trusts? Can they be exciting and stimulating? Can they be fun?

Planning an estate involves arranging for clients' assets to go where they want them to go after their death. That involves finding out not only who are their chosen beneficiaries but how to get the funds and properties to them over the possible objections of other claimants, such as former spouses, self-avowed lovers, self-proclaimed bastard sons, surprise creditors, and black-sheep relatives—let alone the tax man. And considering the constantly changing status of clients—new spouses, new children, new creditors, and so on—and the equally constant alterations in inheritance laws and estate tax laws, accomplishing clients' objectives is no easy task.

On one occasion a careful young man retained an attorney to draw up a will for his mother. She wanted to be sure her black-sheep nephews got nothing and that her son got it all. The attorney carefully drew up the will, then just as carefully had the son witness it.

The mother died. The black-sheep nephews got everything! A witness to a will cannot inherit anything under that will, and the son had been a witness. The lawyer goofed.

So the son sued the lawyer. At last the lawyer looked into the law books rather than guessing, and there he found that in the eyes of the law his client had been the mother, not the son, who had selected him. So since the son had no standing to sue the mother's lawyer, the lawyer escaped scot-free.

This is not the way to practice estate planning. First, you would soon lose all your clients, and second, it is nerve-wracking to be sued for your errors, even if you win. Estate planning, if you study it, can be a source of immense satisfaction. Imagine a client smiling when you explain the tax savings you have planned, and imagine the beneficiaries' gratitude when their bequests are passed to them with a minimum of hassle.

And imagine your own pleasure when you collect your fee. Fees are usually measured in part by the size of the estate rather than solely by your hours worked, so the fee sometimes may be a welcome bonus in addition to your hourly rates.

I have seen lawyers estimate the size of the estate of each living client, estimate the fee based on a percentage of the estate, estimate the client's life expectancy (taking into consideration drinking and smoking habits and known physical weaknesses), and then discount the fees to the present date—all to estimate the lawyer's own net worth! A little much, I'd say, and as a client I don't think I'd be pleased to hear of my personal discounted value to my lawyer.

Estate planning need not consist only of dreary calculation and recalculation. It sometimes can be enlivened by bringing other family members into the decisions—planning several interrelated estates at once, perhaps for several generations in the same family. And it may encompass considerations other than money, including the emotional value of the family home, the protection of loved pets, and provisions for favorite charities.

One enterprising estate planner, Kirsten Alpren of New York, who had been Miss Denmark of 1976, opened a business making videotaped wills. These are to be played back to the family or others after the client's death, and they sometimes enable a client to get a load off his or her chest, explaining from a TV screen to someone exactly why they got nothing.

Why not?

Next to real estate, criminal law, and estate planning, divorce is the most likely type of business for the general practitioner. Divorce business in the big cities is dominated by "bombers," who use almost any means to win a case. Bombers resort to private detectives, raids on love nests, possibly the hiring of gigolos, uncovering previously hidden marriages, and the exploiting of any soft spot usable for marital blackmail. But bombers are careful to stay within the law.

Divorce cases typically begin with your client saying, "We want a friendly, simple little divorce." This attitude, without any help from you, probably will change gradually. Your client, once sad and loving, will become outraged and want blood. And money, once said to be only a modest issue, now becomes the focal point.

Because of the volatility of divorcing parties, most bombers collect their fees up front—perhaps $7,500 and up as an initial payment. And more is paid in advance after that is used up. General practitioners, if they know the clients in other connections, may not be so hard-hearted. But advance payments are desirable if not essential. Some divorce clients are emotionally disturbed or just plain loco. Some clients reconcile, even if briefly. Others are prone to become angry with the lawyer, then fire him or her. And an occasional divorce client commits suicide. So retainers in advance are the general rule.

Should you try to salvage the marriage? Yes, because that is the fair and ethical thing to do. But don't feel disappointed if you fail. Probably only about 5 percent of marriages survive a visit by one spouse to a lawyer. This is not surprising when you consider that about 50 percent of all marriages today end in divorce.

The financial aspects of divorces are the stickiest. Taxes are one, because a deduction for the husband is taxable to the wife and vice versa. But determining finances in the first place is even more difficult. Does one spouse have hidden assets unknown to the other? Whose is the joint bank account? What about pension plans? Fringe benefits? Stock options?

There has been much publicity about no-fault divorce and equitable-distribution laws. These have not done much to ease the trauma of divorce. And women, who now receive a better initial split of the property, get less future support and are left largely on their own with no choice but to try to transform themselves magically from housewives to wage-earners. In fact, about two-thirds of divorcing women did not work regularly before the divorce and now must do so. Women with young children and older women are left in a particularly precarious financial position. You'll find emotional tugs in some of your cases.

One law firm is said to have advertised, for male clients and perhaps in jest, that

We are able to offer divorce services in a package deal with a new will. Our chartered pilot is standing by ready to take you to Santo Domingo or Port-au-Prince, perhaps with a new "friend." We will provide you with documents to take with you for your divorce there, and if necessary the documents which your children can use to bring their own suit against their mother.

If any of your divorce clients want to remarry immediately, try to slow them down. A rush from the courthouse to the altar can result shortly afterward in a rush from the bedroom to the courthouse. One solo practitioner, a kindly soul if a bit unrealistic, advises divorcees to sleep with new lovers for three nights but abstain from sex so that the pair can get to know each other and to calm the trauma resulting from the recent divorce. Marry only after that, he advises with a wise look.

While we are considering divorce practice, perhaps you should glance over your shoulder at your own marriage. Should things go badly and you yourself become involved in a divorce, your spouse may get part of the value of your new law practice!

Closely akin to divorce is the palimony suit, made famous by attorney Marvin Mitchelson in a case involving actor Lee Marvin. Mitchelson had done warm-ups in garden-variety divorce cases, such as a $2.5 billion divorce suit against Saudi arms dealer and financier Adnan Khashoggi. Actually, Mitchelson has never won a palimony case in court, although Lee Marvin was ordered by the trial court to pay his girlfriend $104,000 for "rehabilitation," something like a result under the equitable distribution laws. However, Mitchelson has made palimony famous and feared, and palimony settlements are often reached by other attorneys.

Mitchelson denies that such settlements are blackmail.

He now is extending the palimony concept by representing a man claiming to be the homosexual lover of the late movie star, Rock Hudson, who died of AIDS. The alleged lover says that Hudson exposed him to that disease and thereby has damaged him; he feels this damage can be compensated for with money.

As a general practitioner, you will be confronted by other novel situations. Maybe a friend's son is arrested, with others, for growing marijuana using a hydroponic method in the basement of his fraternity house. An employee is fired by his supervisor for refusing to participate in a parody of the song "Moon River" that ended by mooning the audience. Your college eating club is sued because it doesn't admit women. And so it goes.

I decided to call my friend Bud Williams, who had been working on the architect's plans for the red-light house, to see how his practice was developing.

"How's your new enterprise coming?" I asked.

"Great!" he said. "I'm getting lots of real estate business. Building contracts and things like that. People heard that I did a good job for Rebecca Trice."

I was curious. "Are you getting any criminal business through your contact with her?"

"No. All I got through her is one case defending her. It's an accident case."

"How would Rebecca be involved in an accident case?"

"Well, it was that old house of hers, before the new one was built. You know, the police raid it once a year at Christmas, just for public relations. They don't arrest anybody."

I was even more curious. "What happened?"

"Well, the police came in the front door and sat down to have a few beers. This out-of-town customer came down the stairs and saw ten or twelve blue uniforms there, and he panicked. He yelled something about having a wife and children and tore right into the kitchen and dived through the window. He hit on the back porch, bounced, and rolled off and fell on a stob. Messed him up pretty good, but nothing permanent."

"You mean he's suing Rebecca?" I asked.

"Yeah. His wife found out about the thing because of the cuts and bruises. So he figured he might as well get the insurance money."

"But what's his legal theory?" I asked.

"Exits! Exits!" Bud said. "He claims that the house was a firetrap with no more exits than it had, and that he wouldn't have been hurt if it had had enough exits to be a safe house. That's just what I told my cousin, the architect. A red-light house has got to have lots of exits—lots and lots of exits!"

◆◆◆◆◆◆◆

A general practitioner must be the most versatile of all attorneys. He or she must be prepared and equipped to take on negotiations involving anything from divorces to dog bites, from tax matters to liability cases. All this requires resourcefulness, patience, decisiveness, and confidence.

If you'd like to be one of those indispensable one-person do-it-alls, you must be prepared, even more than the specialist, to keep up with constantly changing laws, moral standards, and legal procedures, with new people and new circumstances every day.

Expecting the unexpected and knowing how to deal with it is an essential part of the general practitioner's weaponry. There have even been occasions when, at slightly different times, an attorney has represented both parties to a divorce and has been able to supply convincing testimony for each of his clients.

Can you shift gears smoothly from real estate to criminal law, from estate planning to house closings? If so, and if you prefer Main Street to Wall Street, where specialization is almost mandatory, you may find general practice exciting, challenging, and even lucrative.

8

LITIGATION
PRACTICE

"My client talks like an idiot and acts like an idiot. Do not be deceived, gentlemen. He really is an idiot."

The members of the jury were bug-eyed. These words came from the defense counsel—about his own client. The counsel was Samuel Leibowitz, a great criminal lawyer who seized on any means of escape for his client, any opening, no matter how small.

If you have an instinct to go for the jugular, to take advantage of every small whim or weakness, maybe you should become a specialist in litigation. Can you, like Leibowitz, get the jury to believe that your client is an idiot rather than a criminal? Can you convince them that the plaintiff's witness is incompetent or a liar? Can you make the plaintiff (or the defendant, if you are the plaintiff's lawyer) seem to be the real villain? Can you, as did one infamous lawyer, deliver an hour-long summation on your knees?

Can you guess which jurors are likely to come to a preordained conclusion? Can you decide how to dress for each particular occasion? Are you a good actor, or would you go to a method acting course for lawyers? Can you laugh or cry at will? Does it offend your sense of dignity to bring a client's wife and children to the courtroom and hope, or maybe suggest, that they cry? Can you tailor your case to fit the place you are in? The kind of people on the jury? Local mores and customs?

Maybe not all these traits are necessary, but many of them are found among litigators. And they can pay off.

Take the location of the trial, for example. Can you fit yourself to that place, as Pennzoil's attorneys did when it sued Texaco?

Here's how it happened. Pennzoil offered to buy Getty Oil Company for $8.9 billion, and Pennzoil's executives were under the impression that Getty had accepted. In fact, Getty officials had celebrated by drinking champagne with their Pennzoil counterparts. Then Texaco came along and offered $10.1 billion, and Getty accepted that instead. So Pennzoil sued.

The case was to be tried in Texas, so Pennzoil immediately hired a real hometown boy for its lawyer. It was Joe Jamail, who dressed habitually in sport coats and high-heeled Texas boots. He had won forty personal injury verdicts of more than $1 million each. He was a man almost unbeatable before a hometown jury, and he orchestrated a hometown strategy.

From the beginning, Texaco played into Jamail's hands. They moved to disqualify Judge Ferris because of a $10,000 contribution from Jamail to Ferris's election campaign; this was after the suit began but before Jamail became counsel. Jamail turned this attack to his advantage by saying, "It's a disgrace . . . [to] smear the judicial system."

A second judge disallowed Texaco's motion.

Jamail set the tone to the jury early. "The question . . . is what . . . your word is worth, what a handshake is worth. [That's] the way I grew up, and the way I am sure most of you did," he began.

He then referred to the "conspiracy between Texaco and a group of New York investment bankers and New York lawyers."

He offered himself in contrast: "I have my own small law firm. I was born here. I grew up here. I went to school here, and I live here."

The stage was set. The verbal gunfight began.

Texaco played it straight. It called several sophisticated Wall Street types as witnesses. One juror later described them as "very pompous. . . . They never looked us in the eye."

Texaco called Marty Lipton to the stand. Lipton, a famous and respected New York takeover lawyer, was asked on cross-examination whether he made a "distinction between just us ordinary people making contracts with each other and whether or not it is a $10 billion deal?"

Mr. Lipton answered truthfully. Probably to Texaco's everlasting sorrow, he said, "Yes, indeed."

Saying that an "ordinary" Texan's handshake is different from a Wall Street agreement got the goat of the Texas jurors. One said later, "My jaw just dropped."

Then Lipton suddenly corrected Texaco's counsel to say that a lawyer in Lipton's office was just an associate, not a partner. One juror characterized this as Lipton reinstating "the caste system." Another said, "Texaco should have left Marty Lipton in New York."

At that point another Pennzoil lawyer, John Jeffers, told the jury that "one of the things that has to be done in this case . . . is to bring that circle of people [New York investment bankers and lawyers] square with the law."

Then, as icing on the cake, Pennzoil subpoenaed Texaco's president, John McKinley. His testimony was straightforward, but Jamail kept telling McKinley to "speak up" so the jurors could hear him, which may have had the effect of making the jurors suspect that McKinley was trying to hide something.

Then, for contrast, Pennzoil called its own president, Hugh Liedtke, to the stand. A great raconteur, he readily "spoke up" without prompting. Mr. Liedtke held the jurors spellbound with tales about his Texas background and his experience as a wildcat oil-driller. There was a Texas smell about him.

Inevitably, there was a Texas verdict: $11.1 billion for Pennzoil, the largest jury award in history!

In retrospect, it looked as if it very nearly was even more Texan. The jurors, apparently while they were considering punitive damages, had sent the judge a note asking whether they should hold Texaco accountable for the actions of Lipton.

Many other factors were involved, of course. But winning this case may very well have turned on Pennzoil's acute awareness that the trial was being held in Texas—not New York or Delaware, but Texas. And the jury came not from Wall Street but from Texas.

There's an interesting sidelight to this story. After the verdict was publicized, the stock-market value of Texaco was quickly reduced by $2.7 billion, but the value of Pennzoil rose only $600 million. Where did the difference go? As James Michaels of *Forbes* said, only half kidding, "It was probably a reserve for what the lawyers will cream off the two companies."

After the verdict in the *Pennzoil* v. *Texaco* case, it is said that one major corporation hastily reconvened a board meeting. At the earlier session a resolution had been passed authorizing the president to "proceed" with an important transaction. At the reconvened session, after a long discussion, the resolution was amended to authorize the president to "proceed with caution."

In *Pennzoil* v. *Texaco* the tactic was to make the defendants seem to be outsiders, conspirators, connivers, shysters, northerners, easterners—people not deserving of mercy.

In the famous *Scopes* "monkey trial," which involved

the legality of teaching Darwinian evolution, Clarence Darrow came up with a classic example of another tactic—making your opponent seem like a fool, someone whose claims should be brushed off as nonsensical or even laughed off.

Darrow called as a witness the lawyer for the other side, William Jennings Bryan, a three-time Democratic candidate for President of the United States and a devoted theologian who insisted that the Bible be read literally. Darrow asked questions, the answers to which necessarily made Bryan seem ridiculous. Some of them can be paraphrased as follows.

When Joshua made the sun and earth stand still, wouldn't one side of the earth have melted?

If all living things not in the Ark were drowned in the flood, were the fish drowned?

When the Tower of Babel was built and God confused the tongues of the people into 500 languages, did they all speak one language before that?

If the earth was built in six days, and the sun was built on the fourth day, how did they have days (evenings and mornings) before the sun was built?

If Eve was made from Adam's rib, where did Adam's son get his wife?

If God made the serpent go on his belly, how did the serpent travel before that?

Darrow's autobiography says that "Bryan twisted and dodged and floundered, to the disgust of . . . even his own people. . . . Bryan had made himself ridiculous. . . . I was truly sorry for him."

Although Darrow technically lost the case, no fine or imprisonment was imposed on his client, and history considers the case a victory for Darrow.

A sad footnote: Bryan, a folk hero to many and a semireligious figure to many more, died five days later near Dayton while taking a nap. He was buried at Arlington National Cemetery. Was he a victim of the courtroom tactic of being made into a fool, a charlatan, and a bigot? Was it crushed pride? A broken heart?

When you are just starting out, you won't deal with anything as large as the *Pennzoil-Texaco* case or as important as the *Scopes* case, but your tactical problems may be just as difficult. A one-person office in a small town can handle cases that would test the resourcefulness of the greatest legal scholar and that perhaps would be beyond the capacity of most Wall Street lawyers.

Consider Jefferson W. Morrow, the attorney for John Ted Wright, who was tried in Jacksonville, Florida, in 1984 for alleged rape of a fourteen-year-old girl. Wright's defense was that the nine-inch size of his penis made the crime unlikely or impossible. Both his girlfriend and his common-law wife testified that lovemaking with him caused his partner to receive painful lacerations, and the examining doctor, Dr. Cleveland Randolph, Jr., testified that the size of Mr. Wright's appendage would cause lacerations but that he had found no such indications on the victim. A photographer testified that the nine-inch length existed in a "flaccid" state.

Mr. Wright's attorney then tried to reinforce his case by proposing successively to have the defendant display the organ itself to the jury, to introduce a life-size wooden replica of the organ, to introduce photographs of the organ made by the photographer who had testified, or to introduce testimony that its circumference was four and a half inches. All this proposed additional evidence was excluded by the judge.

The jury convicted Wright, who appealed. The three-judge panel of Florida's First District Court of Appeals affirmed the trial judge's ruling about the additional evidence on the grounds that the "probative value is substantially outweighed by the danger of unfair prejudice, confusion of issues, misleading the jury, or needless presentation of cumulative evidence."

In this instance attorney Morrow was faced with tough questions of proof, highly technical considerations about admissibility of evidence, and delicate judgments as to the emotional impact on the judge and jurors of his every action. And he could not risk causing the victim to cry again. Nothing more difficult was presented in *Pennzoil-Texaco* or in *Scopes*. Perhaps their implications and consequences were more far-reaching, but the difficulties were no larger.

All litigators have their little tricks to get impressions across to the jury. Like Jamail in Pennzoil, it is common for litigators to tell a witness sharply, "Speak up so the jury can hear you," as if to imply that the witness is trying to muffle a harmful answer.

Our now-familiar William Howe of Howe & Hummel was said to have once placed professional actors in a courtroom to impersonate a defendant's sorrowing mother and wife. Once a young woman with a baby sat sadly at one of Howe's trials, apparently related somehow to the defendant. As Howe gave his summation, the woman pulled out one of her breasts and began to feed the baby.

The great Clarence Darrow once put a lady's hairpin down the middle of his cigar and, during his opponent's summation, smoked the cigar until three-fourths of it was a long ash, mesmerizing the jurors; while awaiting the fall of the ash, they heard nothing of the opponent's summation.

A cousin of mine told me that opponents seldom objected to any evidence Uncle John offered, for if it were excluded, he would walk past the jury box and mumble only for their ears, "They don't want you to hear it," leaving the jurors to wonder what was being hidden from them.

Such actions infuriate judges and rightfully sometimes bring contempt citations, but they and many innovative counterparts persist. Litigators are inventive and sometimes diabolically persistent.

What are most litigators really like? A tax lawyer told me they are like Neanderthals. A corporate lawyer, after a couple of drinks, was more explicit. He said that litigators cannot let anything go unanswered and find it equally difficult to agree with anything.

He added that there are two types of litigators, like two breeds of prize dogs. One type is like a Doberman Pinscher, he said. If you make even a passing social remark, the litigator will instinctively slash at it like a Doberman, first at an arm and then at a leg, in and out, in and out, until you are cut and slashed head to toe.

The other type, he said, is like a pit bull dog. A chance remark is locked onto, like an arm. The litigator gnaws at the arm, hangs on it, tugs at it, twists it, and grinds it until the arm is shapeless. He or she hangs on to his first piece of flesh forever, never changing targets. There is no release.

The corporate lawyer said maybe the urge to be a litigator is a primal urge.

Maybe.

To balance the viewpoint, I relayed this description to a litigator. He laughed. "I knew that was a corporate lawyer because he took so many words. I can describe corporate lawyers with just two words: *hot air.*"

My friend George Leonard, formerly with the U.S. Department of Justice and who had opened his own law firm in Washington, once told me about the following episode involving a litigator of the pit bull type mentioned above, who gnaws on the same point and won't let go.

An agronomist had testified as an expert witness and said that his tests showed that the plaintiff's walnut grove had been damaged by fumes from the defendant's factory.

Cross examination by the pit bull-type litigator then proceeded in part as follows.

Q: How can you be so sure that it was the factory fumes that damaged the walnut trees and not something else?

A: I could tell by walking among the trees. I learned that directly from them.

Q: How could you learn that directly from them?

A: Well, after you have worked and lived with trees as long as I have, you get a lot of information passing back and forth, from you to the tree and the tree to you.

Q: Just explain that to me.

A: Well, you can kind of communicate with the trees, find out what's pleasing them and what's not.

Q: (Shouting) What's that? You say you can communicate with the trees? You mean you can talk with them?

A: I didn't say that, sir. I said I can communicate with them in the sense that I can perceive a great deal. I have lived with them. I have nurtured them. They are not mute beings. They can express their feelings.

Q: So you mean they can talk?

A: In a sense, yes. We understand each other. You might call it talking.

Q: Can you talk with other kinds of plants or just walnut trees?

A: You can talk with any kind of plant in the way I mean.

Q: Have you ever talked with a buttercup?

A: Well, yes, in my own way.

Q: What did you say to the buttercup?

A: Well, I was trying to find out whether the soil suited it, and I got an answer.

Q: Is it something like talking to yourself?

A: No. When I talk to myself, I already know the answer. So question and answer both come from me. When I talk to the flowers, I get answers from them, or vice versa.

Q: Can you talk to birds and animals in the same way?
A: That's not my profession, but I have a good relationship with birds and animals, and we can communicate.
Q: What animals do you talk to mostly?
A: Well, everyday animals like dogs, cats, canaries, and so forth.
Q: Have you ever talked with a giraffe?

The summation to the jury hardly mentioned the defendant's factory. It dwelled instead on the remarkable expert witness who claimed to talk all day with flowers and birds and other animals and himself and even a supposedly mute giraffe.

George Leonard didn't tell me what the jury decided. But gnawing on the same point can pay off.

If you do become a litigator, is it because you are fulfilling a primal urge, as someone has said? Litigation has origins consistent with that theory.

Trial by ordeal in some form was prevalent in parts of Europe into the eighteenth century. It might involve walking barefoot over coals or holding a red-hot iron or walking through a fire. The Normans in England had earlier introduced *trial by battle*; professional champions represented disputants. In criminal cases the accuser personally fought the accused; the latter, if he were defeated but survived, was promptly hanged. It was wise only to accuse someone smaller than you.

Today's litigation, although it still has brutal aspects, is an improvement over these earlier systems. But maybe you are inclined to become a litigator because of a primal urge.

If you decide to become a litigation specialist, be sure to keep yourself aloof from your client's business. Be impersonal. Remember that it is your client that has gotten into court, so he or she has a propensity for trouble. Don't be dragged in.

Lawyers have been sucked into trouble by their clients ever since the beginning of the practice of law in the

English-speaking world, or at least since the Highway-man's Case. That case occurred in 1725, when two high-waymen entered into a partnership agreement to do busi-ness on Hounslow Heath. There they relieved several gentlemen of watches, rings, and other paraphernalia. One of the robbers sued the other for an accounting of the plunder.

Instead of ordering an accounting, the court had *both* plaintiff and defendant hanged, according to Professor Wil-liam L. Prosser, of torts fame. It also very nearly hanged the lawyers. The court found both lawyers guilty of collusion with their clients and in contempt. Each attorney was fined 50 pounds, and one was "transported"—sent to a penal colony.

Professor Prosser says that the accounting for profits was thus not allowed.

An even sadder ending, if that is possible, befell attorney George W. Ridenour, Jr., who was convicted in 1986 of helping his client, Jake Butcher, a Tennessee banker, con-ceal $26.5 million from the Internal Revenue Service. Just hours before his twenty-year prison sentence was to begin, the lawyer shot and killed himself.

Rogers & Wells did legal work for the firm J. David & Company and continued to represent it even after some of the partners began to suspect the client of fraudulent deal-ings. But the lawyers had become too involved with the client. When J. David & Company collapsed, Rogers & Wells itself was sued by various victims and in 1986 had to pay $40 million to settle its claims.

William J. Fallon, now remembered as "The Great Mouthpiece"—the title of his biography—was another modern-day lawyer who became too involved with criminal clients. He was the attorney for, and intimate of, such crime figures as Arnold Rothstein, Nicky Arnstein (the husband of Fannie Brice), and other racketeers and underworld figures.

Fallon was probably the most colorful criminal lawyer of his day. Countless beautiful women passed through his life;

they knew he was irresponsible and fickle as he frittered away his large earnings on higher and higher living. Ultimately, due to his zeal to protect a criminal client, he was indicted for jury bribing and went on the lam. He was later captured and brought to court.

Fallon defended himself in a famous trial during which the bribed juror's wife claimed that Fallon had tried to make love to her, which seemed irrelevant. The imaginative lawyer-defendant somehow dragged in the love life of William Randolph Hearst, which also seemed irrelevant, but after all this Fallon was acquitted. Immediately after the acquittal, he telephoned several ladies, telling each that she was the first to hear the news, and then he went to a speakeasy to celebrate. He died of high living, insolvent.

If you take on clients like highwaymen, or Fallon's crime figures, or persons charged with crimes such as racketeering or drug dealing or white-collar offenses, be sure to collect your fee first. Remember, these people supposedly stole from someone else; they might happily steal from you.

But remember, too, if the client pays you in cash, that you have to report to the federal government any cash payment of $10,000 or more. This may later lead prosecutors to call you as a witness to testify about the bundle of cash the client had. You yourself could be accused of laundering it.

So insist on a check—but deposit it immediately to lessen the odds that it will bounce. That is better, but there is still a hitch. The federal government has the power under some circumstances to seize a criminal's assets, including all the assets at the time of the crime. So in some cases the prosecutor can seize your fee and could possibly hail you before a grand jury to explain why you are getting such a check and on what terms.

Being a criminal lawyer requires you to become as wily and resourceful as your clients. Indeed, one book for criminal lawyers contains a chapter entitled "Protecting Yourself." If litigation, criminal or otherwise, excites you, however, and if you like the theatrics and strategic demands of it, by all means go that route.

Gaining experience in litigation with an experienced lawyer is a good idea before you hang out your shingle. But some lawyers plow right into litigation with no previous experience. Robert Kleinman did this after his graduation from Fordham Law School; he brought suits against large corporations and the City of New York with no hesitation and won most of them. If he runs across a new problem, he just calls a friend to ask for advice and then sues away.

There is plenty of litigation for a start-up practice. Civil case filings in the federal courts now number over 270,000 per year. Yes, there *are* that many new federal cases, and there must be many times that number of civil case filings in the state and local courts—plus criminal cases. It's a big, wide-open field. So just make up your mind to do a good job. If you know your client, know your case, know the opponent, know the court, know the community, and understand jurors, you'll be a winner.

Near Casper, Wyoming, people work outdoors and are partial to guns. One Saturday night last year at a late hour an easterner went into a local bar there and got into an argument over a bar girl. He began firing a 30-30 rifle into the crowded bar. His seven wild shots hit only one person, just superficially; then he was disarmed by some cowboys.

He was tried for attempted murder of the man who had been pinked. His lawyer, a local old-timer, knew the prospective jurors and eliminated all except deer and elk hunters, who pervaded the area. After a brief trial the lawyer leaned both arms on the jury-box rail and spoke to the jury in brotherly tones.

"The first thing you ought to do is teach this poor fellow how to shoot. If he was standing six feet from a bull elk and the elk was paralyzed, he couldn't hit it. If he was trying to kill anybody, no better'n he kin shoot, he must be too crazy to stand trial."

The jury acquitted the man with the recommendation he go back East.

◆◆◆◆◆◆◆

The courtroom lawyer is the most publicized, romanticized, and fictionalized character in the business of law. Like Perry Mason and Clarence Darrow, he or she combines an instinct for the dramatic with tenacious attention not only for the fine points of the law but for human attributes and weaknesses as well.

Truly successful litigators are often, in essence, highly proficient amateur psychologists. Their ability to predict human responses matches their legal talents. Performing in a courtroom is sometimes much like acting on stage. You have to wear the right costume for the occasion, tailor your case to fit the place where the trial is being held, and adjust your style to the kind of people on the jury and to local mores and customs.

Litigation is not a specialty for the shrinking violet, the cloistered scholar, or the inherently timid. But for those who seek drama in life, litigation can be very satisfying— even if you solve no cases by tricking an unsuspected but hysterical murderer into shouting out a confession in court.

9

TAX PRACTICE

"The rich don't pay taxes—they pay smart tax lawyers to figure ways around the IRS." So goes the conventional wisdom.

But consider the case of David Mahoney, chairman of the board and president of Norton Simon. Mahoney is an important and respected figure in financial and business circles. His tax advisers once included the corporation's large internal tax staff, a major New York law firm, a national accounting firm, and a former commissioner of Internal Revenue—a high-powered parcel of consultants.

Yet they ran up a huge income tax bill for Mahoney; at the same time he lost a fortune in real money.

This is a simplified version of what happened in one year, using hypothetical numbers. First, Mahoney had stock options. He could have bought Norton Simon stock for $1 million that at the time was worth about $2 million. His advisers said that the Internal Revenue Code did not include such paper profit as taxable income, so he could exercise those options. He did so and briefly had a $1 million paper profit.

He was happy—perhaps for the last time that year.

Then his advisers said that further study had revealed that the paper profit of $1 million got into a complicated category called a "tax preference"—a term familiar to rich people who use tax shelters and that technically fit Mahoney's situation. The advisers said that the profit would be subject to a "minimum tax" of 10 percent.

Mahoney must have paled; but he still had a $1 million paper profit, less 10 percent.

Then the stock market dropped. The stock that had cost $1 million and that was once valued at $2 million was now worth only $500,000. His advisers said that if he sold, he would have an actual loss of $500,000 out of the $1 million cash he had paid. But this real loss would eliminate the tax preference that had caused the extra tax.

So he gritted his teeth and sold the stock at a real loss of $500,000.

Then the advisers proudly told Norton Simon's directors that they had cured Mahoney's tax problem. The board was compassionate. Without Mahoney's knowledge, they granted him some additional stock options to replace the ones he had exercised and lost money on.

His advisers studied this move. They then said that, although Mahoney hadn't known about the grant of the new options, they had been granted within thirty days of his sale of the stock at a loss. This made the transaction a "wash sale" under the tax law, so the loss didn't count any more. Mahoney's now-vanished paper profit of $1 million had cost him $100,000 in extra income taxes because of the tax preference plus a real cash loss of $500,000 on the stock he had sold. He now was out $600,000 in cash and had nothing to show for it.

Then the board, apparently contrite that its surprise grant of options had unintentionally wrecked Mahoney's tax plan, decided to solve all his financial problems by paying Mahoney's taxes for him. It voted $733,000 for this, including Mahoney's legal fees. His advisers again studied this and then told Mahoney that if the company paid the $733,000 for him, that would be taxable income, and he would have to pay federal taxes on that amount. When the company reimbursed those taxes, he would owe tax in turn on that tax, and so on to infinity.

And then there were the state taxes.

At the stockholders' meeting the next spring, Norton Simon hired Mortimer Caplin, former commissioner of Internal Revenue, to explain all these maneuvers to the widows, orphans, aged couples, and other shareholders. According to eyewitnesses, Caplin was highly unsuccessful. By the end of his explanation he seemed as hopelessly lost and confused as the widows, and orphans he was addressing. Mahoney had listened intently to Caplin's explanation and glared disbelievingly and perhaps with hostility at the dais where Caplin stood.

Wilma Soss, a stockholder gadfly, said, "I've never heard of anything like this." It's a safe bet that very few of the others had either.

But don't let this tale discourage you. If Mahoney's problems had been simple, his tax advisers would have been subjected to more criticism. But the more complicated the problem is, the less likely it is that you'll ever be criticized, no matter how well or how poorly you handle it.

Most lawyers don't go into tax practice without experience in that field. To tackle tax questions just out of law school is dangerous, although it is possible. The usual sequence is law school and then a year or two with an experienced tax lawyer (or the Internal Revenue Service) and, anytime after that, your own practice.

Most tax specialists practice not alone but with partners as part of a firm; it is often a three-, four-, or five-person firm. This is because tax questions usually are related to commercial or financial transactions and therefore occur where commercial or financial law is being practiced—involving contracts, real estate, trusts and estates, and the like. So there is fallout business for the tax specialist from his or her partners.

But occasionally a lone practitioner specializes in tax successfully. John F. Costello, the in-house tax counsel at RCA, resigned to practice tax law alone. To hold down costs, he set up offices in his two homes, in Centerport, New York, and Lenox, Massachusetts. He divided his work days between the two offices. He took on all types of tax cases, including reorganization questions, pension plan matters, and tax fraud cases.

Costello has said, "I like tax practice better alone. A lot of partners tend to be negative about every new idea, so I think I'm more creative by myself. In addition, I don't have to waste time explaining something to a partner who might not understand it anyway."

Of course you have to have a good deal of self-confidence to adopt John's attitude, but if you know you're good, why not?

But most of your problems as a start-up tax firm will be less complex. A good portion of them initially will concern questions about personal taxes, such as "Can I take a deduction for my wife's car if she uses it in charity work?"

You'll get a lot of queries about charitable contributions; people like to take big tax deductions for property they no longer want. *The Wall Street Journal* recently checked a number of universities and charities about non-monetary gifts; the results will make you sit up. Unwary charities have been stuck with "racehorses that eat more than they win, questionable Picassos, and building lots that are sliding into the sea. . . . [One of the horses] ate about $7,000 worth of oats and never won a race."

Leaky boats are favorite contributions, as are vacant buildings. In every case, the donor intends to claim a deduction far greater than the value or the cost of the item or items contributed.

Don't kid yourself. The IRS is wise to all this. Donations of property have to be accompanied by an outside appraisal if they are valued at more than $5,000; the charity has to report the actual sale price if the property is sold within two years. There is a plethora of penalties, so warn your clients to take it easy when cleaning out the attic and sending the stuff to the church.

Some of your well-meaning acquaintances will ask if you do tax returns. You'll eventually find that tax returns are not profitable compared with other work; you'll recommend an accountant to them. But it's a good idea to accept tax-return business at first because you learn a lot about taxes that way and pave the way for additional business. In effect, you get a client attached to you. A small assignment may lead to bigger tax questions or maybe to some nontax business if you have time or if somebody in your office specializes in other matters.

Preparing tax returns is seasonal work, largely confined to March and April. But other tax work, including questions about pending transactions and audits of tax returns, is year-round business.

The personal tax business can be big. In 1985 about 100 million personal income tax returns and 3 million corporate returns were filed. Of the personal returns, some 1.5 million were audited by the Internal Revenue Service. Some of this work, of course, is better suited to mass producers such as H&R Block, but much of it is a good door-opener for a start-up lawyer. And some of it inevitably ends up in court. The tax court alone has about 75,000 cases pending!

Normally a client should not deal with Internal Revenue Agents directly; clients tend to do and say surprising things during tax audits. Better that the lawyer should handle the audit. You should tell the client so, emphatically.

An Internal Revenue agent once called my friend Dr. Malcolm Moley, a dedicated surgeon, and asked for an appointment with Mal's lawyer or accountant to audit his previous year's tax return.

"I'll just do it with you myself," said Mal. "Come to my office on Monday."

The Internal Revenue agent arrived and asked for the expense records and bank statements.

"What is that on your face?" replied Mal spontaneously.

"What's on my face?" asked the agent.

"That spot. Come here by the window and let me get a closer look," said Mal.

"What do you see?" asked the agent, alarmed.

"We'd better go across the street to the hospital. They have an outpatient operating room there with good lights. Follow me."

Across the street, into the hospital, up an elevator, and the panicked agent was operated on!

The spot wasn't malignant. The audit hadn't occurred. Mal's lawyer learned of the episode and quickly had the audit moved to his jurisdiction, with a different agent.

There are two areas in particular where a brand-new law firm will get lots of tax questions: personal and company retirement plans, and tax shelters.

First, retirement plans. The last decade has seen a many-fold growth in the kind and number of these.

Your client may be faced with enough decisions to take you a week to work through. If he retires, should he elect to request a lump sum and income averaging for tax purposes, or should he go for an annuity and pay full taxes as he collects? Should his estate or his wife be the beneficiary under the plan? Can he save taxes by leaving his unreceived retirement funds to his children or grandchildren? If the plan contains company stock, should he take the stock and avoid the tax on any appreciation? Often the employer has several plans, and decisions have to be made for each. And maybe the client has an Individual Retirement Account (an IRA) or a Keogh plan, too.

If you're lucky enough to find a client with his own business but who hasn't yet started any retirement plans, you have found fertile ground. Say the client is a professional writer, a doctor, or a small storeowner. You can become a hero by saving him or her money for retirement—and send out a big bill to boot.

As for tax shelters, be careful. The 1986 Tax Reform Act supposedly killed them, but it really didn't. Your clients will be deluged with proposals. A typical one might say, "Save five dollars in taxes for every dollar you put in." Only a small fraction of these are bona-fide investments with bona-fide tax advantages. Most are crackpot schemes. Some are outright crooked.

Even a seasoned business executive can get taken in by the con men who sell these shelters. In the famous Homestake drilling scandal, which bilked some $100 million from its victims, nonexistent oil wells were sold to an amazing blue-chip list of executives and professionals.

The fraud was expert, the brochures were attractive and expensive, and the entertainment was lavish. Questions were answered by showing the proud target someone else's oil rig and saying it was his. The sales were accomplished via free jet trips to the West, and so on.

Among those ensnared, for hundreds of thousands of dollars in some cases, were Jack Benny ($300,000!), Barbara Walters, Liza Minnelli, Candice Bergen, Barbra Streisand, Walter Matthau, Bill Blass, Thurmond Munson, Sen. Jacob K. Javits, U.S. Court of Appeals Judge Murray L. Gurfein, Secretary of Defense Thomas S. Gates, Admiral Chester Nimitz, New York Superintendent of Banks Muriel Siebert, and New York Attorney General Nathaniel L. Goldstein.

If you have the patience to read long lists, continue. If not, skip the next paragraph.

The suckers' list also included top officials of United States Trust Co., Carter Hawley, Hale Stores, Bethlehem Steel, J. Walter Thompson, Lazard Frères, Eastman Dillon, Western Union, Procter and Gamble, Wertheim, R. H. Macy, Manufacturers Hanover, Heublein, Goodyear, PepsiCo, Warner-Lambert, L. F. Rothschild, Salomon Brothers, Gannett, First Boston, Citicorp, Singer, NCR, Merrill Lynch, Time, International Paper, General Electric (thirty-five officers), Reynolds Securities, Dean Witter, Walgreen, ITT, Tribune Co., and partners from the following blue-chip law firms: Dewey, Cravath, Lord Day, Sullivan & Cromwell, Davis Polk, Debevoise, Arnold & Porter, Shea Gould, Gibson Dunn.

One other prominent name in this long list of victims is none other than that of our friend David Mahoney, chairman of Norton Simon.

Punishment? Retribution?

If seasoned investors can be so easily outsmarted by a tax shelter promoter, what chance has the little guy? Promoters in the last few years have packaged tax shelter deals for the masses—even registered them with the Securities and Exchange Commission. These supersalesmen go up to assembly-line workers and get them to invest all their savings (say, a few thousand dollars) and sign a note. The promoters then tell them they can now claim back all the taxes they paid in the last three years and that they won't have to pay any more taxes in the next several years.

Sound good? Of course it does. Thousands have bit—and their savings are now gone. The IRS has disallowed the schemes, but the poor trusting souls are in debt for taxes to an extent they may never work out of. Favorite schemes involved movie films, master recordings of music albums, fake ministries, breeding of horses and even rabbits, energy "cogeneration," and leases of anything and everything.

The government is fighting crooked shelters hard, and the new 1986 law will help some. A special unit of the Justice Department is investigating fraud possibilities in shelters involving maybe hundreds of thousands of investors. And the IRS is performing civil audits on a massive scale. In 1985 it audited 137,640 returns showing tax shelter deductions; it asserted deficiencies and penalties of $2.4 billion!

The IRS is also going after the promoters themselves; it assessed $54 million in penalties in 1985 against promoters of 136 abusive shelters. Injunctions were taken out against 42 of them. The IRS recommended 213 cases to the Justice Department for prosecution and is considering criminal action in 335 others. The result has been 10 trial convictions and 39 guilty pleas, as well as prison terms averaging 38 months imposed on 46 promoters. One promoter tried to shoot himself when a sizable St. Louis Cardinal first baseman announced his intention to investigate the whereabouts of his vanished investment personally.

If a promoter comes into your office and asks you to help him with a tax shelter offering, be doubly careful—lawyers can go to jail, too. Included in the 213 cases mentioned above that the IRS recommended for criminal prosecution were 44 professionals: 13 CPAs, 15 other accountants, and horror of horrors, 16 lawyers!

Although your tax practice may initially involve mostly personal taxes, you will soon enter the arcane world of corporate taxes. Here you will find corporate mergers, takeovers, foreign tax credits, international tax treaties, offshore insurance companies, tax havens in the Cayman Islands and elsewhere, and all the esoteric tax matters that you read about in the business section of your newspaper.

These can be tricky. One man was told by friends in the golf club locker room that his business would cause great estate tax problems, so he should sell it to his daughter.

He should not give it to her, he was advised, because of gift taxes. So he went to a local general-practice lawyer and sold the business to his daughter, taking back a little stock, a note, and a little cash. He then played golf for the next three years and bragged to his pals frequently about his farsighted tax program.

Then he was audited by the IRS, which said that the transaction had not been a sale but had been a special kind of reorganization. The cash he had received was not a capital gain but was "boot" and a dividend taxable at ordinary rates. The note was really stock, so the interest could not be deducted, and the note when paid would be ordinary income in full. The tax basis of the business was still as it had been previously and had not been increased by the "sale." The price had been too low, and he owed a gift tax on the difference. He owed interest on the back taxes and a penalty for failure to file the gift tax return.

Next time this man will look for a tax specialist like you—even a start-up one.

The complexity of the tax treatment of simple transactions makes tax lawyers seem goofy to other lawyers. Almost universally they are regarded as having strange minds. I believe it is the laws, not the lawyer—but who's to say?

Are tax lawyers strange? Possessed? Eccentric?

One New York tax lawyer, Hiram Knott, is noted for having accumulated huge piles of papers in his office; some of them are several years old. An executive of Tele-Communications once came into Knott's office for a conference and lost his briefcase there. Knott, the client, two secretaries, and the receptionist searched; it was finally found neatly lodged between two stacks of old papers.

Henry deKosmian, another tax lawyer, was, like Knott, both an accumulator of large piles of papers and a very heavy cigarette smoker. Henry would often dash off, forgetting a cigarette burning on his desk. He probably set a nationwide record for desk fires. Two of these were of such magnitude as to require outside help to extinguish them.

Single-minded?

But then, there was the litigation lawyer who left his wife in a gas station restroom and later tried to call her at home from his hotel room to say good-night. No tax lawyer ever did that.

Don't get overconfident about your knowledge of taxes. Maybe you wouldn't have let the man sell his business to his daughter and get into so much tax trouble. Or maybe you could have kept some of those people out of the phony tax shelters or helped the St. Louis Cardinals' first baseman.

But remember that the famous Pennzoil-Getty deal, before Texaco came crashing into it, had some of the best legal minds in the country working on it. There were experts by the hundreds; all of them charged enormous fees. As part of the agreement in principle, they planned for Getty Oil to buy back all its stock owned by the Getty Museum. They realized much later, and with considerable shock, that the tax law makes Getty Oil a "disqualified person" that could not deal in any way with the Getty Museum and that any dealing between it and the museum was prohibited as "self-dealing."

The tax penalty alone, if the deal had been consummated, would have been $2 billion! The nation's top experts had very nearly caused the nation's largest tax penalty.

One day I had lunch with one of David Mahoney's tax advisers, the ones who had "helped" him with the stock option problem at Norton Simon.

"Did they pay your bill that year, after all the trouble?" I asked.

"Oh yes," the adviser said. "There was no trouble. All our advice was sound. Dave did lose a little money—well, maybe a lot—but that was because everybody did the logical thing. They were dumb. They should have known better than to try to be logical. You can't work that way."

"Well, did Mortimer Caplin get paid for trying to explain the deal to the stockholders?"

"I'm sure he did, and he deserved every cent he got. He really saved the company's tail on that one."

"Why?" I asked. "Nobody understood him. Even the press was confused, and the papers said the explanation was incomprehensible."

"That's not the point. The explanation was incomprehensible. But that's because the *law* was incomprehensible. If I'd said the same things, I'd have been booed. Caplin saved the day just because he was a former commissioner of Internal Revenue. People thought he must know what he was talking about. That's worth a fortune in this racket."

Corporate taxes, personal taxes, retirement plans, tax shelters—you can concentrate on any of these or, more likely, be called on to perform your wizardry in a huge array of tax-related situations. In the area of corporate taxes alone you may be asked to contend with mergers, takeovers, foreign tax credits, international tax treaties, tax havens, and many arcane embellishments on our nation's extremely complicated tax structure.

Because of this tangled web, tax lawyers have gained a reputation for being a bit addled. Many attorneys who specialize in less exotic matters consider their tax-lawyer colleagues eccentric, if not somewhat possessed. If you have to deal every week with confusing, contradictory, sometimes literally incomprehensible rules and regulations, you yourself are bound to seem a little confused or confusing at times.

But simply because of the complexity of the tax laws, you'll always be in demand to help trusting clients, personal or corporate, find their way through the tax maze. Like death and taxes, tax lawyers have become one of the few certainties in day-to-day life in America.

10

CORPORATE PRACTICE

Corporate Lawyer: Hello.
Bank Client: We've got some new business for you. We are lending a company called OPM $2.5 million dollars, and it's to be secured by some lease payments to OPM of $57,000 a month by Rockwell International. Will you review the documents for us?
Corporate Lawyer: Yes. I'll dig right into it. Thanks a lot.

This was an ideal conversation for a corporate lawyer—it involved the kind of business every corporate lawyer dreams about. It was exhilarating.

Now consider the following telephone conversation, which occurred just a couple of weeks later.

Bank Client: You fool, OPM is bankrupt, nonexistent. That loan is a total loss.
Corporate Lawyer: But it was secured by a Rockwell lease, and Rockwell is like gold. I read that lease. I studied every word.

Bank Client:	You idiot, some crook at OPM substituted a phony page in the middle of that lease showing the rent at $57,000 a month. That phony page was in our copy. The payments really are only $1,000 a month. And you, you dimwit, you didn't call Rockwell to check it.
Corporate Lawyer:	But I wasn't supposed to do that. That was a credit check for your credit department.
Bank Client:	Like hell it was. Our insurance carrier is bringing suit against your law firm for $2.5 million for malpractice.

Maybe those weren't the exact words. But that's the gist of the two recent calls; the story is true. And those two conversations, a couple of weeks apart, show the joys and pitfalls of corporate type practice.

Who are corporate lawyers?

I'll tell you how litigators and tax specialists see corporate lawyers. Corporate lawyers generally have expensively decorated offices, very plush. They spend long lunch hours at expensive restaurants. They are very social; they attend all the important parties and often appear (alone or with their spouses) in social columns. They don't go to football games or watch football on TV. They generally have one good-looking spouse at a time, usually more than one spouse over the years. Their line of business doesn't require much intelligence. They don't work very hard. They are a menace to their partners because they tend to cause their own firms to be sued.

In addition, according to the other lawyers, corporate lawyers often fantasize that they are entrepreneurs as well as lawyers; gratuitous business advice gushes from them. When clients are highly successful at business, corporate lawyers sometimes believe that they are really the ones who made the deal. Business people are just their agents, they think.

That's how tax lawyers and litigators perceive corporate lawyers.

These perceptions contain a kernel of truth. But there is a good deal more to be said about corporate lawyers.

A corporate lawyer's day can involve lots of different kinds of problems. An executive wants a new contract with stock options, phantom stock, and a golden parachute. A corporation wants to issue stock to the public and needs to register it with the Securities and Exchange Commission. A bank wants loan papers reviewed, as in the above telephone calls. A corporation wants to acquire another corporation or all its assets.

A corporate president's wife's maid turns out to be an illegal immigrant, and the wife wants the corporate lawyer to "rush" the immigration process and to tell the immigration officials that the wife is a friend of President Reagan. Often the corporate lawyer is involved in eight or ten such matters in a day, jumping from one to the other.

How much legal work is involved in such things? I asked several corporate lawyers to tell me the number of hours they spend on various types of matters. Of course the hours vary widely, depending on circumstances and clients' dictates. But here is a sample list of hours of work when your client is a corporation.

MATTER	LAWYERS' HOURS
Executive's employment contract	5
Lease of a store	40
Stock option plan	20
Golden parachute agreement	10
Mortgage on a factory	15
Unsecured-term bank loan	20
"Revolver" bank loan secured by receivables	20

MATTER	LAWYERS' HOURS
$1 million common stock issue	400
$100 million common stock issue	1,000
Forming a new corporation	5
Merger of two small corporations	100
Annual report to a state	1
Annual report to the SEC	30
Proxy statement for shareholders	30

To give you some perspective on this, remember that a typical corporate lawyer might work 1,500 to 1,800 hours a year. Unusual ones work 3,000 hours.

If you can represent one or several corporations in such matters, your billings may be very large over the course of a year. Imagine that amount of time billed at $100 an hour—or $200. And don't forget that your secretary's time can be billed separately; some firms do it that way.

Some clients generate more work than others. Charles A. Hubner, a highly regarded corporate executive, has collected on three large golden parachutes in two years. Raiders keep buying companies where he works. He is a lightning rod.

As to the securities part of the practice, some of it arises under state laws, but most of it originates in the Federal Securities Acts of 1933 and 1934. These require certain periodic reports by publicly owned companies. But—and this means more profits for lawyers—they require a registration statement whenever there is a sale of securities to the public. Since the underwriter that sells the securities for the company, and the company that issues the securities, and sometimes the accountants, company officers, and directors, and maybe even the lawyers, may be liable for errors or misstatements in the registration statement, a great deal rides on your expertise and care.

Your role under these laws could be as counsel to the underwriter. Or you could be counsel to the issuing company. That's much more likely for a start-up firm. Most underwriters, at least the substantial ones, have long-established relationships with large old blue-chip firms and are unlikely to give any worthwhile business to a newcomer.

But the issuers may include companies that, like you, are just getting started. A new computer company, a new toy company, a new department store chain—any or all of these might need a lawyer to do their side of the work if they are going to sell securities to the public.

A few words of warning. First, your payment may be chancy; new companies often can't afford standard legal fees unless the offering of securities is a success. So your fee may in actuality be contingent, whether you agreed to that or not, unless you get cash up front or unless you take stock yourself. You may have heard tales of lawyers taking stock and becoming millionaires, but there are many more instances where the stock turned out to be worthless. Remember my Uncle John and his drawer full of worthless stock certificates, all accepted in payment of legal fees.

Second, you have potentially great liability if there are errors in the registration statement and related documents. Even a firm so august and mighty as Wall Street's White & Case felt the repercussions of such errors in the registration materials filed by it for National Student Marketing; White & Case itself was sued and decided to settle. The legal costs in defending White & Case were estimated at over $10 million. You can get insurance against this kind of liability, but the cost is so high that it may make the work unprofitable.

Even if you don't do securities-type transactions, there is still plenty of other work to do for corporations. For instance, there are about 160,000 companies incorporated in Delaware alone. Each one needs annual franchise returns, stockholders' minutes, directors' minutes, and qualifications to do business in other states. All that means an enormous amount of routine paperwork. Some companies will need pension plans and pension trusts. A few may need employment contracts with their executives and incentive compensation plans. Some will need trademark registrations, which will be easy for you to learn about.

Perhaps franchise agreements or license agreements are involved. If your client is opening even a single McDonald's Restaurant franchise, think of all the agreements involved.

A company may be involved with purchase contracts, long-term sales contracts, and leases for its factories or stores. And perhaps its products or services have to be walked through a federal agency—maybe the Food and Drug Administration or the Federal Trade Commission or the Federal Communications Commission.

Don't hesitate to tell your clients that they need your services. Tell them of problems they might not have foreseen. They want you to do that—it's good for both of you.

Once I attended an annual meeting of U.S. Industries in Wilmington, Delaware. The chairman of the board, John I (no period) Snyder, Jr., a man not noted for his patience, described a proposition to the shareholders.

Then Snyder said, "It requires a 50 percent vote of those stockholders present at this meeting."

A stockholder jumped to his feet. "It needs 50 percent of *all* the stockholders," he shouted, "including those *not* present."

"Let's take a brief recess," said Snyder.

Then he seized his in-house corporate counsel, Sandy Kaynor, and an independent counsel, Dick Moser of Patterson, Belknap, by the arms and dragged them to a corner.

"Which the hell is it?" growled Snyder. Maybe it was more of a snarl.

"It's what the stockholder said," said Moser, "50 percent of all the stock, not just 50 percent of what's here."

"Why the hell didn't you tell me in advance?"

Moser, without a blush or a pause, turned to Kaynor and said, "Sandy, you should have asked me about that."

To this day Kaynor tells how Moser adroitly shifted Snyder's anger onto Kaynor, and then Kaynor laughs and says, "That Moser was a crafty one." Kaynor sure wished Moser, the outside counsel, had *volunteered* the answer in advance.

You should voluntarily tell clients everything they might need to know—within reason.

Some corporate lawyers overdo this. They make themselves obnoxious by spewing out unneeded and unwanted advice and by overworking every situation involving any possible legal question. The latter type of attorney can leave a bad taste in a client's mouth regarding lawyers in general.

A friend of mine, Jack Parker, formerly vice chairman of General Electric, complains of corporate attorneys who give him unwanted advice and then bill him for it, or who do much more work on a transaction than he thinks is needed. He has asked me the same question a number of times, never remembering, or maybe not caring, that he has asked it before.

"Do you know the definition of *a damned shame*?" he asks.

"No," I say.

Jack then says, "It's a busload of lawyers running off a cliff with one seat empty." He then laughs uproariously.

On the other hand, some executives think lawyers are less evil than investment bankers. An executive of a large cable company, while making a billion-dollar-plus bid for the Westinghouse Group W cable system, commented about the huge array of investment bankers involved in the deal: "I must say that, after having met all those investment bankers involved in this deal, my opinion of lawyers has gone up. The lawyers are doing something—or trying to do something. The investment bankers just hang around in herds. I suppose lawyers aren't so bad after all."

I mentioned earlier that the corporate lawyer tends to claim credit for the business successes of a business client. Ironically, this fantasy has its counterpart in the businessman's tendency to blame the corporate lawyer if the business deal goes sour.

John Horan left an established law firm to help start up a corporate law firm. One of his first client firms asked him to prepare an employment contract for a newly recruited sales executive.

The president of the client firm said to Horan, "Don't let that executive get away. Give him anything he wants, because he is top flight and we have got to have him. And do it by tonight. We want him to sign later today, and then we'll have cocktails and a celebration dinner. So get things rolling!"

"But," said Horan, "I need to discuss with his lawyer our termination rights and our management controls. What if he doesn't meet sales quota? What if he cuts prices below our costs without permission? What if he commits us beyond our manufacturing capacity? What if he gives information to a competitor? What kind of expenses can he run up?"

"Forget all of that junk!" shouted the president. "We want him today, so forget all of that legal baloney and do a very simple contract, and have it ready in two hours. That's an order!"

So Horan did just that. The contract was signed. There were cocktails and dinner, as expected.

Six months later Horan, disbelievingly, learned that the president had just told the board, "Our vice president of sales has fallen down completely and has sold only about 50 percent of his projections, but our factory has turned out twice as much as he sold, and the extra inventory is piled up in warehouses. In addition, the expenses in his department are out of sight, and they have no records to support the expenses."

"Why don't we fire him?" a board member asked. "His salary is one of the highest in the whole company."

"We can't," said the president. "The damned lawyers didn't put anything in the contract about his performance, and it says that he is entitled to the salary and business expenses for ten years, come what may. I think we should sue the damned lawyers!"

On reflection Horan said to me, "I wish I had written the company a letter at the outset, setting forth my recommendations and then the instructions under which I had to work."

He is right. He should have recorded these facts.

You should, too, in your corporate practice.

Litigation and tax lawyers, despite the complexities of corporate law, tend to regard corporate lawyers' practices as not demanding much ability. They think of corporate lawyers instead as social gadflies, always trying to make an impression, particularly on clients.

It is probably true that corporate people try harder than others to impress clients, particularly by entertaining them. Tax lawyers don't bother trying to make an impression; they are preoccupied. And litigators sometimes seem to deliberately insult clients. But corporate lawyers always mind their p's and q's with clients.

Lavish entertainment often is thought to be the order of the day. This is all right; entertain if you want to. But be sure to prepare carefully.

Bill Rooney, in the process of starting his own law practice, called a prospective client and invited him and his wife to dinner at an expensive restaurant where Rooney was unknown. On the morning of the day of the dinner, Rooney's wife discovered that she had lost her credit card, a "satellite" card that Rooney had obtained for her. She conferred with some other housewives and on their collective advice telephoned the credit card company to report the facts.

That night, after a flashy and very expensive dinner, Rooney grandly called for the check, initialed it, and handed his credit card to the captain. After some minutes of polite talk at the table, Rooney noticed the maître d' approaching.

"May I speak to you privately, sir?"

"What is it?" said Rooney, feeling flushed with power from the atmosphere and the meal. "Just tell me what you want."

"It's private, sir. Would you step over here a minute?" asked the maître d'.

"I told you," said Rooney gruffly, "tell me right here what you want!"

"Well, all right, sir," said the maître d' in front of the client. "This is a stolen credit card!"

◆◆◆◆◆◆◆

Like all legal specialities, the field of corporate law has acquired a certain reputation in the legal community. Many lawyers view corporate attorneys as somewhat smug ladies and gentlemen who do business in plush offices and live rich but dull lives, and whose names often appear in society columns.

Is there any truth in this? Like all clichés, this one is partially true. In reality, however, corporate lawyers are not homogenous but comprise as many different species as any other field of legal specialization.

Corporate law requires a keen knowledge of many areas of business, from drawing up employment contracts replete with stock options and a golden parachute to acting as counsel either to the underwriter or to the issuing company in a securities registration. Any incorporated company requires a wide range of legal services, including quarterly and annual reports to the SEC and stockholders' and directors' minutes, and many will need trademark registrations, franchise agreements, license agreements, and other contracts, reports, leases, and papers too numerous to list. If corporate life—and dealing with corporate executives—appeals to you, the possibilities are endless.

11

WOMEN IN THE LAW

"Frailty, thy name is woman!" wrote William Shakespeare around 1600.

That opinion wasn't new in the seventeenth century; it remained virtually unquestioned for another three hundred years. It even had the support of the United States Supreme Court. In 1873, Justice Joseph B. Bradley wrote for the majority in the Supreme Court decision *Bradwell* v. *Illinois*. He held that Myra Bradwell, being a woman, had no constitutional right to become a lawyer. Justice Bradley wrote,

> The nature and proper timidity and delicacy which belongs to the female sex evidently unfits it for many of the occupations of civil life. . . . The paramount destiny and mission of women are to fulfill the noble and benign offices of wife and mother. This is the law of the Creator.

Only now, in the latter part of the twentieth century, can you, if you are a woman, freely enter the practice of law. No longer are you thought to be too frail.

The way is open for you to start your own law practice, alone or with others, full or part time, however you like.

In 1970 about 8 percent of all law students in the United States were women. In 1980 about one-third were women. Now the level seems to have stabilized at about 40 percent. There are probably about 100,000 women among the nation's 750,000 lawyers; most of these female attorneys are under the age of forty-five.

These figures are reflected, of course, in the larger law firms. In 1984 a *National Law Journal* survey concluded that 30 percent of all associates in the country's hundred largest law firms were women. This is about a pro rata for law school graduates, adjusting for the pre-1980 years of small female enrollment. About 5 percent of the partners in the same firms are women. Perhaps this figure also is understandable when you consider the minuscule female enrollment in law schools before 1970.

By the end of this century there may well be almost as many female lawyers as males in the legal profession.

A fifty-fifty split is the opinion of William Falsgraf, president of the American Bar Association. Falsgraf, a partner in the Cleveland firm of Baker & Hostetler, predicts that there will be 1 million lawyers in this country by the year 2000 and that half will be women. He also says that as a result the legal profession will become "more ethical and humane." Perhaps he was a little carried away; possibly not.

But what of women starting their own practices? Although various surveys indicate that many do so, often on a part-time basis, one hears very little of them. Why?

The New York Times published an article in 1985 entitled "Women in the Law: Many Are Getting Out!" Five women interviewed for the article had been associates at established firms and had left their jobs, *none* to start her own practice. The article described a course for unhappy lawyers called Career Options for Legal Professionals; it noted that fifteen of the twenty-three students were women. Presumably these were all employees, not self-employed. The article listed some of the jobs to which former lawyers—male and female—had turned: jingle writer, real estate broker, theatrical agent, restaurant owner, art dealer, public relations executive, photographer, actor, journalist, management consultant, salesman, stockbroker, literary agent.

Notably absent from the list of women lawyers' jobs was starting their own law practice. If women lawyers are not starting their own law firms, what are they doing? Some leave the law; what of the others?

Carol Kanarek, a New York search consultant, says they are going to the government and to banks, to insurance companies and to large corporations. Possibly there the atmosphere is less adversarial, the hours are regular, the income is assured, and the positions seem more desirable than a start-up practice. Kanarek points out that as they progress upward in government, banks, insurance companies, and large corporations, these women will determine which law firms get the legal business.

Maybe being the client is the better of the two worlds. A male lawyer might be abusive to a female lawyer whom he supervises. But no male lawyer in his right mind is going to behave in an unwelcome fashion—flirtatious, patronizing, or otherwise—to a female who gives him his legal business. She's the boss.

Moreover, female clients are presumably less likely to be sexist in selecting their counsel. That may bode well for you if you are a woman and start your own practice.

The Philadelphia firm Morgan, Lewis might have unknowingly served as a model for the *Times* report described above. In 1982 it lost 10 of its 29 women associates, most often in their fourth year of work; the firm frantically sponsored a series of fancy lunches hosted by its partners for the remaining 19. It lost 17 of them shortly after the lunches.

A 1984 survey by the Maine Bar Association seems to

verify the *Times* report. It demonstrated that 48 percent of women lawyers said they would "think twice" about becoming a lawyer again, compared with 40 percent of the men.

When one looks at the reasons given by women for leaving the law, it becomes even more surprising that they tend not to start their own firms. The reasons are generally related to pressures of one kind or another from their superiors or fellow workers—pressures that need not exist in one's own private practice. These include

- the adversarial nature of the work

- time demands that inhibit any personal life

- petty nonsense issues raised by other lawyers

- indirect pressure to choose a workaholic husband

- the lack of individual significance in the job

- becoming "defeminized" to fit the job

- sex discrimination in salaries and promotions

- overwork, merely because it is expected

- the desire to have a family

- the desire to do something else such as to write, at least part time

Why leave the law for these reasons? Why not start your own practice—perhaps with one or more women like yourself? Pick a field in which you are comfortable, adversarial or nonadversarial as you like. Set your own hours, but coordinate them with those of the other women in your office. Write a book or take up acting in your spare time. Combine the demands of your profession with your desires for a family and the demands of the family. All this is possible—it's your choice.

Of course, some men too want a flex-time professional life, but less often than women.

Your new practice could consist of anything from a part-time practice from your home to an office-sharing arrangement with others to a formal partnership, perhaps with one or two other women or men, and a clear understanding of hours and obligations.

The 1984 survey by the Maine Bar Association showed that 23 percent of the female respondents practice law on a part-time basis, compared with only 13 percent of the males. It's true that some areas of the law, such as many kinds of litigation, cannot be easily adapted to part-time work. But your own part-time schedule is not necessarily inflexible, and usually you can go full time during a crisis. With careful planning and communication, work can be shifted back and forth between part-timers.

You may not make as much money that way. But you can have the kind of life you want without having to give up your profession to do it.

Of course, a number of women went to law school for the wrong reasons in the first place. Some were swept up in the enthusiasm of the women's rights movement and envisioned a quick rise to individual prominence. Others were altruistic; they saw the law as a way to bring about social reforms. Still others went because law school became almost a fad among women in the 1970s. Many of these really didn't know what to expect from real-life law practice.

A second group went to law school for the *right* reason—a suitable and desirable career—but changed goals after marriage and childbirth. For some of these women, perhaps law now *is* the wrong business, and they should change.

A third, large group of women are dedicated lawyers. They work the same hours as men and still find time to have families, write books, and follow their personal pursuits. And some of these have started their own law practices with much success.

Susan Owens went to the University of North Carolina Law School, then married a professional baseball player. When he was "farmed out" to a minor-league team in a small town in the state of Washington, she opened her own office there—alone. She was quite prepared to follow him up the baseball ladder to larger towns. She would probably have opened a one-woman law office on Wall Street if he had made the Yankees.

Lynne Z. Gold-Bikin, a highly regarded divorce specialist, didn't exactly start her own firm; she bought it! Lynne had been recruited by a Philadelphia firm to open a new Norristown branch for the firm. When the branch turned out to be not as profitable as had been expected, she purchased the branch for $50,000, which she raised by placing a second mortgage on her house. She added a woman partner and three associates. The new firm now has billings of nearly $2 million annually. The initial retainer for a divorce case is $5,000, and the fees are based on hourly rates of $100 to $200 per lawyer. Lynne explains her success in part by saying, "I'm damned good." She also has the valuable personal experience of being twice divorced.

Congresswoman Geraldine Ferraro, the 1984 Democratic nominee for Vice President of the United States, graduated from Fordham Law School, then carried on a private practice from her home from 1960 to 1974, when she went into government.

Two women in Poughkeepsie, Laura Zeisel and Kathryn S. Lazar, left their jobs at prisoners' legal services, nonprofit organizations, and opened a law partnership to do litigation; one partner would specialize in class actions for migrant workers and the other in prisoners' rights litigation. Their motives were a mixture of altruism and need for more income. Later they split up; Zeisel joined an environmental firm and Lazar joined her husband in a new start-up general-practice firm. Both are still successful.

In San Francisco an all-female firm, Schapiro & Thorn, specializes in divorce law. One partner technically inherited some of the practice from a retiring male lawyer who had a younger woman partner, but in substance they created the firm as it is now. One of the other women lawyers was a nurse before attending law school; one is a former actress. All three female associates raise children while working. Of sixteen female employees, including bookkeepers and secretaries, ten work part time.

There is also an all-woman firm in Washington, D.C. Solomon, Tinkham & Robinson concentrates on real estate, probate, and corporate work. Tommye J. Tinkham has been quoted as saying they might consider bringing in a man, but only "later on."

Fanny Holtzmann was the only woman to graduate in the Fordham Law School class of 1922. She immediately opened her own office in New York as a sole practitioner, turning down an offer from a law firm to run a branch office. Capitalizing on contacts in the entertainment world that she had made as a part-time law clerk during law school, she quickly built a thriving entertainment practice. Her clients included Clifton Webb, Noel Coward, Fred Astaire, George Bernard Shaw, Gertrude Lawrence, Somerset Maugham, Darryl F. Zanuck, and John Gilbert.

She was also a business adviser in that glittering world; in later life, she became active in public matters involving the UN and Israel's creation. Her most noted legal case, which was orchestrated by her in London, was the libel case against M-G-M concerning the film *Rasputin*, in which she represented the Russian royal family and helped obtain a satisfactory settlement.

As was noted earlier, Fanny hired as an associate lawyer a former partner from the law firm where she had clerked while in law school. When you open your own practice, how would you like to hire your old boss?

Even presumably rich investment bankers can be jealous of women lawyers. "Vivian Gentleman was the lawyer on the other side in one of my matters," said my investment banker friend Ernie Greeff, "and she is a superb lawyer. She practices alone from her home in Westhampton." He looked thoughtful and then added, "I bet she makes a bundle—maybe even more than I do."

He looked worried.

Mia Lancaster is a beautiful model. She wanted to bring a lawsuit but was unable to find a suitable lawyer—at least not one she could afford.

What did she do? *Time* magazine told the story on August 9, 1982, accompanied by a picture of Mia modeling a bathing suit.

Self-Help Model
Suing well is the best revenge

If you really want to get even, get a lawyer. Despite that standard advice representing oneself in court, Mia Lancaster could find no lawyer whom she thought willing and able to press her charges against her former boyfriend. So she argued her own case. A Manhattan jury was impressed: it awarded her more than $1 million, which so far as courthouse buffs could recall, seemed to be the largest damages ever won by someone representing himself. Presiding Judge Joseph Modugno was impressed too. Said the judge: "A remarkable achievement."

Lancaster, 28, was suing Tyrone Kindor, 38, who she says promised to marry her. Instead, Lancaster testified, he absconded with the young model's $11,000 life savings and other personal property, including her modeling portfolio. In 1975 she discovered that Kindor had invested some of her

money in the modeling career of Margaux Heming-
way. . . .

Moreover, because of Kindor's earlier treatment of her,
she told the court, she became emaciated, contracted acne,
lost hair and developed emotional problems that "bordered
on insanity." . . .

Lancaster read an evidence textbook and compiled countless bulging gray folders of correspondence, depositions and
affidavits. . . . The jury awarded her $1 million for that
charge and $21,000 for the loss of her property and savings.
. . . Lancaster is so pleased with her performance that she
has applied to New York's highest court for permission to
take the bar exam without going to law school.

Mia had started her own law practice against over-
whelming handicaps—no money, no clients except herself, no law school training, no license to practice law.

It's not quite a lawyer's story, because she never went
to law school, but Mia Lancaster demonstrated what a
woman can do, even alone, if she wants to practice law.

Maybe Mia Lancaster proved the contention of Flo
Kennedy, a black female attorney: "A woman must be
twice as good as a man in order to be thought half as
good. Fortunately, this is not difficult."

By the way, whatever happened to Myra Bradwell,
of whom the Supreme Court in 1873 said that her
"paramount destiny . . . [was] to fulfill the noble and be-
nign offices of wife and mother. This is the law of the
Creator"?

As fate would have it, Myra Bradwell did not become
the first woman admitted to the Bar in the United States.

That honor went to Belle A. Mansfield of Iowa in 1869.
Iowa law provided for admission to the Bar of "any white
male person," but she somehow convinced an Iowa court
to declare that this statute did not mean, by negative
implication, to deny admission to females. Quite a twist;

a stunning victory! Belle A. Mansfield spent the rest of her life as a professor at Iowa Wesleyan.

Although both Myra Bradwell and Belle Mansfield passed the bar examinations on their first try in 1869, neither had attended law school. Bradwell had studied law in her husband's office in Illinois, and Mansfield had studied law in her brother's office in Iowa.

The first woman graduate of a law school was Ada H. Kepley of Illinois. She graduated in June 1870 from the Law Department of Chicago University (not related to the present University of Chicago). She initially was denied admission to the Illinois bar but then was admitted in 1881 and practiced law thereafter with her husband. The Law Department of Chicago University, which had been established in 1858, was "declared to be also the Law Department of the Northwestern University" in 1872 and eventually was merged into the latter university with all alumni "hereby made alumni of Northwestern University Law School." Thus, Northwestern can rightfully claim the first woman law school graduate, many decades ahead of some venerable law schools of the east coast. Harvard admitted its first woman in 1950.

Back to Myra Bradwell. By the time she fought her case to the Supreme Court, where she lost, she had already established *The Chicago Legal News*, a weekly paper devoted primarily to judicial and legislative matters. She continued this after the Supreme Court decision and became perhaps the most influential woman in Illinois in various reform movements.

Even the great Chicago fire of 1871, which burned almost all her possessions, did not slow her down. She merely stood in Lake Michigan so that she herself would not be consumed by flames, then resumed printing the *Legal News* temporarily from Milwaukee.

Myra Bradwell was so busy with these other things that she did not reapply for admission to the bar, after the earlier denials. In 1890 this fact was brought to the attention of the Supreme Court of Illinois, and it was pointed out that the general public regarded her as the country's best-known and leading woman lawyer, unaware that Illinois had never admitted her. On its own motion, the Court admitted her to the bar *nunc pro tunc* as of the date of her original application in 1869. She is the only person ever admitted to the Illinois bar on the court's own initiative.

It is ironic that neither Myra Bradwell nor Belle Mansfield practiced law themselves. They had become too involved in other things by the time they were admitted. They did, however, pave the way for the thousands of women now practicing law and for those to come.

Could Shakespeare, despite his remark about "frailty," have had doubts that women are frail? Perhaps he was ambivalent, at least as far as women in law are concerned; perhaps he even foresaw the entrance of women into law practice.

In *The Merchant of Venice* Portia disguises herself as a male and acts as a lawyer for Antonio, an impoverished merchant. When Shylock claims his pound of flesh, Portia does not go into a frenzy of motions and appeals and denials, as a male lawyer might have done. Instead she very adroitly agrees, in her argument before the Duke of Venice, that Shylock can have his pound of flesh. But, she adds gently, he can take no blood with it.

The clever Shylock is thus outwitted.

A feminist wag has said that Shakespeare was forced to use a woman lawyer for this episode because a male lawyer would have dragged the case through years of pretrial discovery and *The Merchant of Venice* would never have ended.

◆◆◆◆◆◆◆

Just over a century ago, the United States Supreme Court held that Myra Bradwell had no constitutional right to become a lawyer because she was a woman. Today, perhaps one-third of all associates in this country's one hundred largest law firms are women. By the year 2000, the ratio may well be fifty-fifty.

Yet today, far fewer women than men start their own law firms. Why? The reasons aren't clear.

Female lawyers stand on equal footing with men when initiating their own businesses. The same qualities necessary for a man to succeed in the sometimes precarious profession of law are needed equally by women—ambition, drive, perseverance, intelligence, a certain amount of charm, and dedication. Perhaps by the year 2000 the number of adventurous women starting their own practices will equal the number of male attorneys who take the plunge.

12

LOOKING TO THE FUTURE

During the last two decades, tremendous changes have shaken our economy and the way it works. The steel industry has lost its status and is in ruins. Big oil has been wracked by megamergers and OPEC's attempts to control prices. Passenger railroads have gone the way of the dodo and the dinosaur. The family farmer is vanishing. The automobile industry seeks government aid to survive. Airlines proliferate, then merge or disappear. The computer is everywhere.

If you start your own law practice, you can assume that just as many changes will occur in the legal profession. Be ready for them if you can.

You can see some changes in the profession now. Will they last? Or are they experiments doomed to end in failure? What other changes are possible or likely?

Between 1983 and 1987 fourteen old, respected, and to outward appearances successful law firms in New York city split up or dissolved. In another business the word *failed* might have been used, but the law business is more professional in tone. The fourteen and the number of lawyers in each were

Greenbaum, Wolff & Ernst (50)
Lovejoy, Wassen & Ashton (20)
Marshall, Bratter, Greene, Allison & Tucker (80)
Casey, Lane & Mittendorf (40)
Poletti Freidin Prashker & Gartner (20)
Hale, Russell & Gray (40)
Arthur, Dry & Kalish (30)
Trubin Sillcocks Edelman & Knapp (50)
Guggenheimer & Untermyer (50)
Surrey & Morse (20)
Schwartz, Klink & Schreiber (30)
Alexander & Green (60)
Sage, Gray, Todd & Sims (80)
Paskus, Gordon & Mandel (30)

None of these downfalls was foreseen. In fact, both Greenbaum and Lovejoy had just signed leases on space in a new luxury building at 101 Park Avenue. Paskus, Gordon was 90 years old. Alexander & Green was more than 143 years old.

What happened? Arthur, Dry was simply absorbed into its principal client, U.S. Rubber, and now is the in-house law department of that company. The other firms dissolved or split up. High rents were a factor. Other firms lured away key partners. Some had made more partners than their business would support. Internecine warfare was often a major factor.

At the same time, a rash of megafirms emerged, largely through mergers but sometimes through internal growth. Branch offices were opened in criss-cross patterns by firms across the country. Foreign affiliates were established. Many firms tried to become "full service," with a department for everything.

Sneaking up also are "five-and-ten" firms such as Jacoby & Meyers (150 offices) and Hyatt Legal Service (200 offices), offering wills, divorces, and the like at low standard fees. Prepaid legal plans are spreading among unions, and legal insurance plans are growing; both now cover 17 million people.

Moreover, in some states there is a movement to allow nonlawyers to be made partners in law firms or to own part of them. Such movements may eventually permit an insurance company or an investment banker or a mass merchandiser to enter the law business. Thus you may someday find yourself competing against Merrill Lynch's own law firm, or maybe against American Express.

Let's look at some of these trends, see how they affect your new practice, and examine other trends that might come later.

First, as for becoming a megafirm: you may have left one to choose a private practice instead. So presumably you have no interest in trying to become a giant—at least not soon.

But have you missed something? And can you compete with the giants in the field? Gigantism is not necessarily profitable. Baker, McKenzie, the country's biggest law firm in number of lawyers, and Finley, Kumble, New York's largest firm in number of lawyers, are not notably successful in terms of income. In fact, Baker, McKenzie finished dead last in revenue per lawyer among the fifty largest American firms in 1984, even though it was several times larger in size than some of them; Finley, Kumble finished forty-third on the list of fifty in revenues per lawyer.

A probably apocryphal story concerns a Finley, Kumble partner who, disgruntled with his earnings, was asked, "Why do some of your partners make less money than the associates at blue-chip firms?"

The disgruntled partner supposedly replied, "Some of my partners aren't qualified to be associates at the blue-chip firms."

Huge size often prevents cohesiveness and coordination. Indeed, not all partners in some of the larger firms have even met each other. The giant firm of Morgan, Lewis & Bockius tried to solve this problem by publishing an annual tome, like a college yearbook, with a picture of each partner and his name, law school, and so on. In this way, at a business meeting you could supposedly tell your own partners from somebody else's partners and from the clients. But one member of Morgan Lewis said that, when asked to submit their pictures, many members aged fifty or sixty or over submitted photographs taken twenty years earlier and could not be recognized from their photographs.

Assuming that you don't want to be a megafirm, do you even need to add departments? Do you have to provide service in additional areas, like the full-service firms?

It probably is not necessary. The most profitable firm in the country, number one on a per-partner income basis, is Wachtell, Lipton, which is not a full-service firm but a "boutique" firm of under one hundred lawyers. Wachtell sticks to its takeover defense business and refuses to be lured by arguments for providing full service.

The full-service firms themselves are showing some shakiness about their decision to take that route. Wilmer Cutler in Washington decided to lop off its wills and estates department because it was losing money. It did so, in a sort of spinoff, even though the executives of its corporate clients needed estate-planning services. It had found no synergism from the extra service.

Similarly, a large Chicago firm "set free" its entire battery of product liability lawyers, letting them take clients, files, and all pertinent materials. These lawyers then established their own smaller firm. The reason? The insurance companies paying the legal bills in product liability cases were insisting on discounted hourly rates.

Divestiture of certain departments may become a general trend for a powerful reason: in-house law departments have grown by leaps and bounds. Probably 20 percent of the 750,000 lawyers in the United States now work on in-house staffs.

These staffs affect full-service firms in two ways. First, they provide internal legal services at a cost well below that of outside firms, thus reducing the volume of work for the outsiders, particularly work of a recurring nature. Second, when outside firms are needed for a special matter, the in-house counsel shops for the lowest cost and the best expertise. The expert is generally cheaper in his field than another lawyer trying to learn that field. The in-house counsel realizes that an excellent tax department in a full-service firm, even the best in town, does not necessarily indicate that the same firm's litigation department is the best. So in-house counsel may assign a tax problem to one firm and litigation to another.

This use of multiple outside firms has the incidental benefit to in-house counsel of strengthening their own position within the corporation. They are, along with other considerations, protecting their turf!

Robert S. Banks, vice president and general counsel of Xerox, has been quoted in *Business Week* as calling some of the largest law firms "huge, unmanaged bureaucracies." He says of his use of outside counsel, "I am the leader of the project, and they work for me. . . . The revolution is still in process!"

Edgar A. Bircher, general counsel of Cooper Industries, says, "We treat outside law firms as boutiques, not as department stores." And Robert E. Bowman, general counsel of Household International, puts it another way: "We look for the best lawyer, not at who is chummy with someone."

Mayer, Brown & Platt of Chicago had handled practically all of Continental Illinois Bank's legal work since 1910. When Raymond Myers was named the bank's first in-house general counsel in 1975, he brought much work inside. He switched to Levy & Arem for real estate, Kirkland & Ellis for venture capital matters, and Sonnenschein Carlin for trusts. In addition, when Continental very nearly collapsed in 1982, Jenner & Block was brought in to help. This upset the Mayer, Brown relationship even further. As this critical bank connection loosened, six Mayer, Brown partners left as a group in 1984 to form a Chicago office for a New York law firm.

Similarly, other banks are loosening their ties to full-service firms. Examples are Chase Manhattan with Milbank, Bankers Trust with White & Case, and others.

What does this mean to you as a start-up firm? You *can* get work from the largest corporations, if you can convince the in-house counsel that you are an expert in a particular area. And you don't have to be full service. The in-house counsel will call you when a novel matter arises too suddenly for their staff to become adept at it, if you are already adept, or when the matter requires immediate attention and the in-house people are all occupied. In this boutique world you *can* compete with the big boys and big girls.

If not diversified by way of departments, if you cannot or prefer not to provide full-service diversification, what about *geographic* diversification? Should you have an office in the state capital? The nation's capital? The nearest big city?

Maybe not. The most profitable firms in the country are not always those with lots of branches.

I once asked a law student whether he would advise a client to marry a lady who had a large potential tax deduction and thus offered financial attractiveness. He replied, "Only if he loves her!"

Businesswise, this was the wrong answer. Too many firms have opened branch offices for "romantic" rather than hard-boiled financial reasons. Some seek the prestige of a Washington office. Some open a Palm Beach office just so a partner wintering there can make a show of practicing law among the rich.

In many cases the firm later regrets its decision. The office, expected to be unprofitable at the start, stays that way. And many lawyers are embarrassed at the thought of closing the branch. That's an admission of failure, or so it appears to them. Many firms today have branch offices operating at a loss, and they suffer on and on in silence.

Clarence Darrow used to say of risk taking: "I never advise anyone to play poker or not to play poker, but I always advise them to keep their limit down." That sound advice applies equally to geographical expansion.

Don't open a branch office with all its expenses unless you can foresee definite, identifiable business. Let's say an existing client wants labor law service in a particular town and you have an associate or junior partner you can station there. If the client pays enough, by all means go ahead and open the new office.

But don't make the mistake of generalizing—saying that a particular city doesn't have enough lawyers, so that you probably should open an office there. This is fantasizing, and nine times out of ten you'll be sorry. Few cities are undersupplied with lawyers.

So as far as branch offices are concerned, don't get involved with them for "love"; do it for money.

Is the same true for overseas branches?

Yes—doubly so. Approach them with the same caution and in the same manner. If a client needs a permanent counsel stationed in Hong Kong, by all means open an office there—if the client will pay enough. Otherwise, don't.

I once had some dealings with a New York law firm that I knew to have only four lawyers, including partners and associates. But I received a letter from the firm one day with those four names on the letterhead. To my astonishment, overseas offices in five countries were listed!

"How do you do that?" I asked one of the four.

"We travel fast," I was told gruffly.

That firm is no longer listed in legal directories, and I

suppose it doesn't exist. I might add that it represented a spouse in a harsh divorce case against a friend of mine. To hear its threats and claims you would have thought it had at least four hundred lawyers, all of them professional murderers, so I guess it was entitled to claim at least five overseas offices, although none was in a quickie-divorce country.

One large and respected firm with a number of overseas branches has for some time been suffering losses in some of these branches. It has touted itself as "international" for such a long time that it is loath to close the losing foreign offices. But the drain has caused it to postpone some hiring of young associates and to delay the usual cash drawings of the partners, even in the profitable branches—a horrible dilemma.

Don't get sucked in. Open your eyes before you enter new territory.

In lieu of full-service departments and geographical branches, why not set up a series of informal alliances with firms like your own? If you specialize in bankruptcy, why not make contact with a tax specialist and say you'll recommend him or her when asked for tax help, if he or she will reciprocate with bankruptcy matters. And consider a similar deal with a firm in the state capital, as well as one in Washington and abroad, if your practice calls for it. That kind of alliance is easy to arrange. Much more important, you don't have to incur overhead or losses, and you can get out of it with a simple telephone call. No firing of people, no paying for terminating leases, no unnecessary paperwork. It can work well.

If you plan to practice alone, similar alliances can be arranged to cover your practice whenever you are out of town. Women who want to practice part time, maybe during school hours, can profit even more than men by such alliances to cover them the other part of the day. It need not be a formal partnership—just the simplest arrangement you can conjure up. Remember that Peter Megaree Brown and Whitney North Seymour, Jr., have an arrangement somewhat along these lines, with separate clients, books, profits, and fees—even separate bank accounts. But the two complement each other, and each covers things when the other is unavailable.

There are other potential areas of diversification that are not yet in vogue but that you might consider. The idea was presaged decades ago in Colorado, Idaho, and Illinois where, as we mentioned, probate judges also owned funeral homes. You could get a package deal on being buried and having your estate handled—at least in the Midwest.

You may not want to combine a funeral home with your estate practice. But there are other possibilities, as long as you guard carefully against conflicts of interest. Consider an investment partnership, led by you, to invest with clients who need the added capital. Think about a real estate broker to go with your real estate practice.

An insurance broker? An insurance underwriter for special risks? A travel agency? A leasing company for office furniture and equipment, including your own? An appraisal company to value estates or to value property for bank loan purposes? A school for business executives interested in basic legal knowledge? A stockbroker? An investment adviser? Think about them all. An agency for temporary office workers might work fine. You can vary your own clerical needs a little to mesh them with clients' requirements.

Or you might even consider setting up an agency that rents out lawyers to other law firms for use in emergencies. A company in San Francisco called Lawsmiths does just this.

Arnold & Porter in Washington set up a separate group to offer financial consulting work, including bank regulatory matters, and another to engage in everything from lobbying to real estate development. The latter group recently completed a $30 million project of faculty housing for the University of California at Irvine.

Borod & Huggins of Memphis publishes a bimonthly financial newsletter and provides investment banking consulting services.

Wickins, Herzer of Lorain, Ohio, conducts executive searches for university personnel and provides other services to colleges and universities.

The three-woman firm of Solomon, Tinkham & Robinson of Washington, D.C., practices real estate, probate, and corporate law. But each of the partners has approached business diversification with great zeal: one has an educational consulting firm on the side, another owns and operates an office park, and the third develops real estate.

Many lawyers maintain a profitable business managing all the financial affairs, investments, budgets, contracts, and other matters for personal clients such as athletes and entertainers. This kind of arrangement can be extended to any client who can afford it.

Kaye, Scholer of New York owns a consulting firm specializing in business in China and is considering a separate real estate firm.

Hogan & Hartson of Washington is a partner in a health care consulting firm.

Howey & Simon of Washington has an economics consulting firm that offers services in antitrust and international trade matters.

Shearman & Sterling of New York affiliated with a consulting firm to offer combined legal and financial advice to banks.

Sutherland, Ashbill of Atlanta is a partner in an environmental consulting firm.

Mort Janklow left an established firm in New York and formed a start-up firm, Janklow & Traum. One of its clients was William Safire, the syndicated columnist who was formerly special assistant to President Nixon and who later wrote a book about him. Janklow represented Safire in a lawsuit with a prospective publisher, William Morrow, and then sold the book to another publisher, Doubleday. Soon he got calls from other writers who had problems with publishers, and he commenced handling these writers for a 15 percent commission. He is now known as a "superagent."

Today Janklow practices law and conducts his writers' agency business at the same time. In 1986 he reportedly made more than $1 million as agent for writers such as Sidney Sheldon, Judith Krantz, Jackie Collins, John Ehrlichman, Daniel Patrick Moynihan, Daniel Schorr, and Nancy Reagan.

Pension planning has become a major field for lawyers, especially since ERISA (Employee Retirement Income Security Act of 1974) became part of our law. Small clients with pension plans now require the services of incentive consultants, accountants, actuaries, insurers, and bankers. Why not provide these services yourself, or some of them? Ropes & Gray in Boston has its own in-house actuaries, and it charges for their time. Maybe you would have to add a small staff to do these things, but that could make the expansion even more profitable if you could charge for them at a markup. Or maybe with a little effort you could learn to be an actuary yourself—it's not that tough. This is a great growth area, and many small firms are making a specialty of it. Don't be afraid to tout yourself as knowledgeable; if you get stuck on something, you can hire a specialist on the sly to ghostwrite plans or answer questions for you.

Alston & Bird in Atlanta formed a separate corporation that performs actuarial services; a client wanting a pension plan can now do "one-stop shopping" with Alston & Bird. It will draft his pension plan, provide required employee notifications, attend to governmental filings and ruling requests, and calculate the actuarial requirements of the plan each year. It might be possible for your firm to go even further than Alston & Bird; you could offer to maintain the records for individual accounts, which would require your investing in computer operations. Theoretically, you also could form an investment advisory affiliate that would assist the clients in investing the funds contained in their retirement plans.

Constructing tax shelters fits nicely with the practice of law. It is wise, of course, not to sell tax shelters to your own clients, not unless they are phenomenal ones. Why not investigate syndicating office buildings, shopping centers, and other real estate? This is perfectly all right.

Or how about a mediation service? You could handle divorces expeditiously sometimes. This form of work has lots of advantages over courtroom litigation, including privacy. Or you could inaugurate a mediation service for small claims. Such a service could be freely advertised on a wide geographical basis, perhaps statewide; it usually needs only the agreement of the parties to proceed. Your fee could be generous, yet still be cheaper than having two lawyers battling it out in court; I'm sure you've heard the old chestnut about two men claiming a cow, with one pulling at the head and the other at the tail, while the lawyers milked her. Your service could fill a great need.

Do you want to really diversify? One lawyer in a small Connecticut town has his legal shingle hanging on a white picket fence outside his house. Inside he practices law, and he also deals in antique furniture.

There is a push in the District of Columbia, North Dakota, and elsewhere to allow nonlawyers to become partners in law firms. This would mean that you could take in as a partner an accountant, maybe a doctor, or even an architect. You could all continue to "do your own things," such as your divorce work, in which you don't need the architect. But you could handle other cases jointly, such as a medical malpractice suit in which a doctor partner could help you evaluate the claims and plan the evidence.

Of course, you might "taint" the doctor partner, so that he could not be a witness. But if you and the architect partner were to work jointly on a new shopping center, probably no conflict would appear.

If nonlawyers can own part of a law firm, why not all of it? Who knows? Maybe someday Sears, Roebuck will try to build the biggest law firm in the world. You could sell your own law firm to Sears for a fortune!

As you travel the road of independent practice, you are going to have ups and downs. Sometimes these will be financial, and the difficulties will be real and severe. But with a little luck and much perseverance, the odds are that you will make it.

Sometimes when things seem blackest, they turn around quickly, and you are amazed that you worried in the first place.

Take John Logan O'Donnell. O'Donnell left the giant firm Cravath, Swaine & Moore and started a new partnership with three other people. Eventually he became well known as a litigator on his own account and began to handle a number of sizable cases in the securities field. One of these was *Lipsig* v. *National Student Marketing*, in which he represented the defendant. He was exuberant about his involvement in such a prominent case—until one fateful morning, which he remembers as being dark and cloudy. On that day he received papers in which the de facto plaintiff's lawyer named as defendants O'Donnell and his law firm and also the law firm Pomerantz, Levy, alleging conspiracy with the company to make a fraudulent settlement. The plaintiff was suing the defendant's lawyers!

O'Donnell said in a weak voice, "I almost wish I had stayed at Cravath and not gone on my own so they would be suing Ralph McAfee and those other fellows down there instead of me."

After considerable litigation, the plaintiff's claim against O'Donnell's firm and against Pomerantz, Levy was held to be spurious, brought purely for tactical purposes, and without merit. O'Donnell was fully vindicated.

On hearing this court decision, O'Donnell said in a strong voice, "Well, maybe it's all right to start a law firm and be on your own."

Then O'Donnell's firm and the Pomerantz firm asked the federal court to impose attorney's fees and expenses against the plaintiff for the spurious pleading—in other words, hourly charges for the time O'Donnell spent defending himself. O'Donnell's claim was allowed by the trial court and then upheld by the Court of Appeals. A special magistrate conducted an evidentiary hearing on the amount of the fees and allowed a total of $672,296.48 in attorneys' fees and $49,210.12 in litigation costs. This finding was adopted by the district court judge.

"It's great practicing for yourself!" shouted O'Donnell. "Otherwise, I wouldn't have gotten sued, and I wouldn't have gotten all those attorneys' fees for defending myself!"

◆◆◆◆◆◆◆

The more things change, the more they remain the same. Success in the business of law, however, seems a more questionable proposition each decade. In recent years, at least thirteen of the oldest, most respected, and outwardly most successful law firms in New York City vanished. Rents are getting higher, clashes of personalities seem more prevalent, and megafirms are becoming almost as common in the legal community as they are in heavy industry and transportation.

For smaller firms things look better. In law as in other professions, less is sometimes more. General practitioners in smaller communities are still doing well. So are specialty law firms everywhere that provide certain well-targeted services to their clients.

There are great advantages to thinking small at first, to proceeding slowly and cautiously. Chances are, once you've struck out on your own, you'll encounter financial problems and emotional trauma. But with a little luck and a great deal of careful planning and perseverance, you're bound to make it, as so many others have.

INDEX

A

Advertising/publicity
  "chasers," 14–15
  direct-mail solicitation, 15
  paid advertising
    billboards, 16, 17
    brochures, 16–17
    discount coupons, 16
    newsletters, 17
    personal visits to prospective
      clients, 17–18
    telephone book
      advertisements, 16
    television ads, 16
    type of, 15–19
    video-tape presentation, 18
  public relations firm, hiring
    of, 14
  self-chasing, 15
  self-publicity, 14
Alpren, Kirsten, 96
Annual retainers, 65
Arthur, Chester A., and political
  sales factor, 19–20

B

Banks, Robert S., 153
Barron's Guide to Law Schools, 4
Belli, Melvin
  on ambulance chasing, 15
  hourly fees and, 63
  partnership and, 50
Billboards, 16, 17
Billing/fees
  annual retainers, 65
  billing policies, sample of,
    64–65
  cash in advance, 112
  in check form, 112
  contingent fees, 66–68
    average size of, 66
    insurance and, 66, 67–68
    mass torts and, 66–67
  and criminal cases, 112–13
  for divorce cases, 96–97
  for estate planning, 95–96
  fixed fees, 60–61
  hourly fees
    adding up your time, 63–64

Billing/fees (*Cont.*)
   of famous attorneys, 63
   record keeping and, 63
   obtaining written agreement
     about, 68–69
   probate fees, 61
   questions to ask yourself, 58
   reasons for escalation of, 60–61
   typical billing rates, 59–60
Bolan, Thomas A., 52
"Bombers," 96
Bowman, Robert E., 153
Bradwell, Myra, 137, 145–47
Brady, Chris, 22
Brochures, 16–17
Brown, Peter Megaree, 6
   partnership and, 50–51, 157
Bryan, William Jennings, 105–6
Buckner, Emory, 82–83
Buckner method, 82–83

C

Carter, Walter S., 6, 43
   "Carter's Kids" and, 43–45
   on partnerships, 49–50
Chase, Nicholas, 7, 50
"Chasers," 14–15
Clients
   attracting clients you want,
     13–15
   getting clients
     entertaining and, 25–27
     from former employer, 22
     through a good reputation, 25
     through recommendations/
       impressions, 20–21
     through social connections, 20
     using yourself as a client, 20
   letting client tell his/her story,
     11–12
   nervousness about getting,
     10–11

   See also Advertising/publicity;
     Billing/fees.
Coale, John P., 15
Cohn, Roy M., 52–53
Competition
   advertising/publicity of, 52
   in estate planning/tax fields, 51
   from large corporations, 52
   lawyer-shopping, 51
   legal service plans of, 52
Connelly, John E. Jr., 23–24
Contingent fees, 66–68
   average size of, 66
   insurance and, 66, 67–68
   mass torts and, 66–67
"Contract associate," 74–75
Corporate legal staffs, 62
Corporate practice
   billing/fees, 130, 131
   corporate lawyers
     litigator/tax specialists' view
       of, 128–29
     other lawyers' view of, 129
   corporate taxes, 123–24
   dispensing of unneeded
     information, 133
   entertainment, 135–36
   executives' view of, 133–34
   potential liabilities of, 131
   role as underwriter, 130–31
   securities, 130–32
   typical day in, 129
   work hours in, 129–30
Costello, John F., 118
Cowper, Steven, 31–32
Cravath, Paul D., 45
   Cravath method, 82
Criminal cases
   avoiding handling of, 13
   handling of, 113

D

Darrow, Clarence, 1–2, 105–6,
   107

deKosmian, Henry, 124–25
Direct-mail solicitation, 15
Disasters
  bar associations' view of, 15
  creating business from, 14–15
Discount coupons, 16
Divorce cases
  advance payments for, 97
  "bombers" and, 96
  effect on women, 97
  fees, 96–97
  no-fault divorce, 97
  salvaging marriage, 97
Doberman Pinscher-type
    litigator, 108

E

Ellis, Tom, 7
Ervin, Sam J. Jr., 12–13

F

Fallon, William J., 111–12
Falsgraf, William, 138
Family partnerships, 47
Felder, Raoul, on husband-wife
    partnership, 47–48
Ferraro, Geraldine, 142
Finnegan, Jay, 7–8
Fixed fees, 60–61
Full-service firms, 152–53
  affect of in-house staffs on, 153
Fulton, Hugh, 21

G

General practice
  criminal cases, 112–13
  daily routine, 93–94
  decisions about entering, 90
  divorce cases, 96–98
  estate planning, 94–96
  palimony suits, 98–100
  versus specialization, 90–93

Gold-Bikim, Lynn Z., 142
Goldman, Ralph C., 6, 23–24
Greenfield, Richard, 2–3

H

Halley, Rudolph, 21
Hamilton, Alexander, 42
Hasler, Tim, 32–33
Holtzmann, Fanny, 143–44
Horan, John, 134–35
Hourly fees
  adding up your time, 63–64
  of famous attorneys, 63
  record keeping and, 63
Howe, William F., 93, 107
Hummel, Abraham, 93
Humor of a Country Lawyer
    (Ervin), 12–13
Husband-wife partnerships,
    47–48
Hyatt Legal Services, 150–51

I

Incorporation, reasons for, 85
In-house law departments,
    152–53

J

Jacoby & Meyers, 150–51
Jacque, Leonard, 15
Jacques, Emile W., 24–25
Jamail, Joe, 102
Jay, John, 42
Jeffers, John, 103

K

Kanarek, Carol, 139
Kaynor, Sandy, 132–33
Kent, Chancellor James, 42
Kepley, Ada H., 146
Kessler, Kathleen, 20

Kleinman, Robert, 113
Knott, Hiram, 124
Koegel, Otto E., 43
Kohn, Harold, 3
Kray, Steven, 52

L

LaGuardia, Maryanne, 6–7
Lancaster, Mia, 144–45
Large firms, 46
Law office
  importance of, 28
  location of, 28–36
    for corporate law practice, 28
    differences in, 35
    large-city practices, 28
    locations that "need" lawyers,
      35–36
    near family/friends, 35
    small-town practices, 29
  scientific organization of, 45–46
Lawyers
  hiring of
    avoiding mistakes in, 81
    choices involved, 81
    creating leverage business,
      81–82
    salaries, 82
  training of
    Buckner method, 82–83
    Cravath method, 82
Lazar, Kathryn S., 142–43
Legal profession
  future of, 149–63
    "five-and-ten" firms, 150–51
    full-service departments,
      152–53
    geographic diversification,
      154–55
    informal allegiances, 156
    law firms, dissolution of,
      149–50
    mediation services, 160

  mergers, 150
  tax shelters, 160
Legal service plans, 18
Leibowitz, Samuel, 101
Leonard, George, 108, 110
Leverage business, creation of,
  81–82
Lincoln, Abraham, law practice
  of, 13
Lipsig v. *National Student
  Marketing*, 161–62
Lipton, Marty, 103–4
  hourly fees and, 63
Litigation practice
  adjusting to trial location,
    102–4
  criminal cases, 112–13
  gaining experience in, 113–14
  keeping aloof, 110–12
  litigators, types of, 108
  origins of, 110
  personality of litigators, 108–10
  questions to ask yourself, 101–2
  Scopes "monkey trial," 104–6
  small versus large firm and,
    106–7
  trial tactics, 107–8
Lloyd, Leona Loretta, 48–49
Lloyd, Leonia Janetta, 48–49

M

Machiz, Larry, 74–75
Mahoney, David, 115–17
Mansfield, Bette A., 145–46
*Martindale-Hubbell Law
  Dictionary*, 42
Mediation service, 160
Megafirms
  competition with, 151
  disadvantages of, 151–52
  diversification and, 153
Mitchelson, Marvin, 98–99
Morrow, Jefferson W., 106–7

Moser, Dick, 132–33
Murray, John V.A., 24–25
Myers, Raymond, 153–54
My Life in Court (Nizer), 63

N

Neel, Henry, C., 38–39, 55
Newsletters, 17
Nizer, Louis
  hourly fees and, 63
  self-publicity and, 14
No-fault divorce, 97
Non-lawyer personnel
  administrative review of, 85–86
  hiring of, 78
  office manager, 78
  paralegal, 83–84
  secretary, 76–79
    treatment of, 79–80

O

O'Conner, Sandra Day, 7
Office manager
  hiring of, 78
  Peter Principle and, 78
  responsibilities of, 78–79
Office space/equipment
  part-time office, 75–76
  your apartment as, 74
  tasks required to acquire,
    72–74
O'Hara, John, 8
O'Hara, Kathy, 34
Owens, Susan, 142

P

Paid advertising, 15–19
  billboards, 16, 17

brochures, 16–17
discount coupons, 16
newsletters, 17
personal visits to prospective
  clients, 17–18
telephone book advertisements,
  16
television ads, 16
video-tape presentation, 18
Palimony suits, 98–100
Paralegal, hiring of, 83–84
Partner(s)/partnership(s)
  as buyer/seller of business, 40
  Carter, Walter S. and, 43–44
  comparison of lone practice to,
    38–39
  as coworker, 39–40
  dispersal of, 51–53
  family partnerships, 47
  husband-wife partnerships,
    47–48
  large firms, size of, 46
  meetings with, 41–42
  nonlawyers as partners, 151,
    160–61
  personality problems of, 49, 54
  as promotion piece, 40
  qualities sought in, 46, 55–56
  as "rainmaker," 40
  sister-sister partnerships, 48–49
  as specialist, 40
  as substitute, 39
  as synergist, 40
  theft by partners, 53–55
Pennzoil v. *Texaco*, 102–4
Pension planning, 159
Peter Principle, office manager
  position and, 78
Pit bull-type litigator, 108–10
  cross-examination by, 109–10
Politics, as sales factor, 19–20
Probate fee, 61
Prosser, Prof. William L., 111
Public relations firm, 14

R

"Rainmaker," 40
Record keeping, and hourly fees, 63
Rich, Stephanie Lueders, 34
Ridenour, George W. Jr., 111
Rooney, Bill, 135–36
Russell, John, 51

S

Salaries, lawyers, 82
Sales factors
  advertising/publicity, 15–19
  "chasing," 14–15
  direct-mail solicitation, 15
  legal service plans, 18
  politics, 19–20
Santarelli, Don, 64
Secretary
  hiring of, 76–79
    opposite sex, 78
    same sex, 77
Seymour, Whitney North Jr., 6, 50–51, 157
Sims, Leonard, 74
Sister-sister partnerships, 48–49
Specialization, versus general practice, 90–93
Spivak, Gordon, 51
Start-up law practice
  billing/fees, 58–68, 95–97, 112–13
  clients, 10–27
  competition, 51–52
  corporate practice, 123–36
  Darrow, Clarence, and, 1–2
  divorce cases, 96–97
  employment breakdown for graduates, 4
  full-service departments and, 152–153
  general practice, 90–113

geographic diversification and, 154–55
informal allegiances, 156
law office, location of, 28–36
lawyers
  administrative review of, 85–86
  hiring of, 81–82
  training of, 82–83
litigation practice, 101–14
non-lawyer personnel, 76–80
office space/equipment, 72–76
partners/partnerships, 38–42, 46–55
reasons for opening, 1–9
tax practice, 117–26
women and, 137–46
Stemple, Gordon, 15
Stuart, John T., 6

T

Tax practice
  charitable contributions, queries about, 118–19
  corporate taxes, 123–24
  experience needed for, 117
  lone practice and, 118
  partnerships and, 117–18
  questions concerned with, 118, 120
  retirement plans, 120–21
  size of, 119
  tax lawyers, eccentricity of, 124–26
  tax return preparation, 119
Tax shelters, 121–23
  constructing of, 160
  representing promoters of, 123
Telephone book advertisements, 16
Television ads, 16
Tinkham, Tommye J., 143

Training of lawyers
  Buckner method, 82–83
  Cravath method, 82
Trial by battle, 110
Trial by order, 110

U

Union Privilege Legal Services,
  18–19

V

Videotape
  presentations, 18
  wills, 96
Volume discount plans, 62

W

Walter, Henry (Hank), 21–22
*Walter S. Carter, Collector of
  Young Masters* (Koegel), 43
Webster, Daniel, 42

Weisfuse, Doreen, on husband-
  wife partnership, 47–48
Williams, Edward Bennett, 7
  partnership and, 50
  self-publicity and, 14
Women
  as clients, 139
  and law school
    first women law school
      graduate, 146
    reasons for attending, 141–42
  as lawyers
    in large law firms, 138
    past view of, 137
    reasons for leaving profession,
      140
    in start-up law practices,
      138–39
    women law students, number
      of, 138

Z

Zeisel, Laura, 142–43

ABOUT THE AUTHOR

Harry F. Weyher is a senior partner in the New York law firm of Olwine, Connelly, Chase, O'Donnell & Weyher. Born in Wilson, North Carolina, he studied at the University of North Carolina and the University of Glasgow (Scotland) before receiving his bachelor of laws degree *magna cum laude* from Harvard, where he was note editor of the Law Review.

He was admitted to the New York Bar in 1950. Prior to joining his present firm, he was senior associate counsel of the New York State Crime Commission. Mr. Weyher is a former adjunct associate professor of law of the N.Y.U. Law School.